JOINING
JESUS
AS A FAMILY

JOINING
JESUS
AS A FAMILY

How to Raise Your Children to be Followers of Jesus

GREG FINKE
SUSAN FINKE

TENTH
POWER

ELGIN, IL • TYLER, TX

TENTHPOWERPUBLISHING
www.tenthpowerpublishing.com

Design by Inkwell Creative

Softcover ISBN 978-1-938840-54-8

e-book ISBN 978-1-938840-55-5

10 9 8 7 6 5 4 3 2 1

To our parents: Marty, Norm, Art, and Jane
When we were growing up,
you took us to church, and taught us the faith;
but it was your lifestyle that was our discipling curriculum.
Thank you for showing us Jesus.

To our children: Amanda, Emilie, and Ellen
It's been a fun adventure growing up with you!
Together we learned how to join Jesus as a family.
Today, you not only know the faith, but you also live it.
And we are so thankful.

TABLE OF CONTENTS

INTRODUCTION

"Do whatever he tells you."

-Mary to the servants in John 2:5

There are many conversations we could have about parenting your children: how to help your infant sleep through the night; how to negotiate with a toddler; how to get your children to stop fighting; how to survive the upheaval of adolescence; or how to help your children process the effects of everything from divorce, to the pandemic, to bullying, to social media, to... the list goes on and on.

Perhaps that's why U.S. parents spend nearly $400 million every year on parenting books and apps.

But if Susan and I were to choose one conversation to have with you that could serve as a foundation for all the others, it would be the one we're about to have: how to raise your children to be followers of Jesus. This book may not address all your parenting questions, but it will provide clarity for how to intentionally raise your children to follow Jesus so their lives will be full of his love, wisdom, purpose, and guidance as they navigate all the other challenges and opportunities they will face.

In a previous book, I quoted a friend who likes to say, "All we can do is bring the water. It's up to Jesus to turn it into wine." That's certainly true when talking about raising our children to be followers of Jesus. Parents bring the "water" of their love, example, and teaching; but, in the end, it is only Jesus who can work the miracle of transformation in a child's life.

You might have recognized my friend's quote as a reference to the wedding at Cana (see John 2). During the wedding, Mary tells Jesus the wine has run out. In response, Jesus tells the servants to fill six large jars with water. And the servants do it. In fact, we are told that they fill each jar to the brim. (Do you think they knew Jesus was up to something?) Then Jesus does what only Jesus could do. He changes all the water into wine. Really good wine.

And so it is as we raise our children. We follow Jesus' discipling plan. We do what he tells us to do and fill each jar to the brim in anticipation. But, in the end, it is Jesus who turns our discipling-water into discipling-wine. There will be days and seasons when, despite our best efforts, the results will differ from what we had hoped, especially as our children mature into young adults and start making their own way. We may look back and worry about what we could have done differently.

But don't underestimate Jesus.

He is faithful and his love endures forever. In short, he keeps the promises he made to our children at their baptism. In fact, he is relentless about it. When his sheep go astray, he goes after them and keeps looking until he finds them (see Luke 15:4). When we worry about them, he assures us, "No one can snatch them out of my hand," (John 10:28). Despite how present circumstances look, Jesus reminds us to focus on the long arc of their life because he has plans for them – plans to prosper them not to harm them, plans to give them hope and a future (see Jeremiah 29:11).

So, let's talk.

Parenting is, indeed, a crazy journey full of twists and turns, good seasons and hard. And it's definitely more an art than it is a science. But that's why it's so important for us to heed Mary's wise advice, "Do whatever he tells you."

Because your miracle is coming too.

How to Use This Book

Don't miss the Discussion Guide for Parents located in the back of the book.

Whether you are going through the book as a group or as an individual, the Discussion Guide for Parents is designed to help you process your insights and, just as importantly, turn those insights into action for the benefit of your family.

Susan and I have prepared online resources to help you join Jesus as a family.

Go to www.dwelling114.org, click the "Training Tools" dropdown menu, and then click "Joining Jesus as a Family." There you will find a number of resources, including a Family Circle-Up Guide.

Look for two bonuses at the conclusion of each chapter.

"Here's the Point" provides a summary of the chapter. "Susan's Snippets" provides one more insight, encouragement, or lesson from Susan as you think about how to apply the chapter in your family.

What if I'm a single parent or a spiritually single parent?

If you're a single parent or a spiritually single parent (that is, you're married but your spouse is spiritually absent, or not a follower of Jesus, or follows a different religion), you face unique challenges in raising your children to be followers of Jesus. However, his promises to you and your children remain the same. Therefore, follow Jesus' plan and pay special attention to chapter 17 where we talk about the value of building a "village" of Jesus-followers for your children.

What if I'm not the biological parent?

If you're not the biological parent but are helping to raise a child – you're a grandparent, foster parent, or guardian – this book is definitely for you too. Thank you for all you are doing with Jesus to raise this precious child. Whenever you read the word "parent," know that Susan and I are talking to you.

CHAPTER 1

MOM AND DAD, HOW HAS JESUS BEEN MESSING WITH YOU?

"Let not your hearts be troubled."

—Jesus in John 14:1

I could see the terror on their faces.

I was somewhere in the upper Midwest having breakfast with a small group of younger dads. The night before, I had given a presentation at their church on my first two books: *Joining Jesus on His Mission: How to be an Everyday Missionary* and *Joining Jesus—Show Me How: How to Disciple Everyday Missionaries.*

They were fired up by what they heard and wanted to talk more. So, they invited me to meet them at their favorite downtown breakfast spot ahead of my flight the next morning. During breakfast, I mentioned that my wife and I were working on a new book.

"What's it about?" they asked.

I finished chewing to give myself a moment to collect my thoughts, "It's about taking what I unpack in the first two books and applying it to raising our families. My wife and I want to help parents intentionally disciple their kids to become lifelong followers of Jesus. We're thinking of calling it, *Joining Jesus as a Family*."

As a group, they stopped eating and looked up at me. I could tell Jesus had just started messing with them. I smiled.

One of them clarified, "Did you say, 'To help *parents* disciple their kids?'"

"Yep," I replied.

And then the table exploded. Everyone started shooting questions at me.

Some were bewildered, "How would I do *that*?"

Some were excited, "How can I get started?"

And some were incredulous, "*Why* would I do that? Isn't that why we take our kids to church?"

Still smiling, I looked around the table and said, "Here's the deal, friends. Whether you know it or not, and whether you like it or not, you're already discipling your kids in what it looks like to be a follower of Jesus. The kind of Jesus-follower you are now is deeply affecting the kind of Jesus-follower your kid will become."

The table got very quiet. Their brains were spinning. It seemed like Jesus was *really* messing with them now. And it was good.

"You see, God designed your little child to watch you, imitate you and become a version of you. That's how discipleship works. So, your lifestyle of faith, for better or worse, is already deeply molding and shaping your child for a lifetime...just like your parents' lifestyle deeply molded and shaped you."

I let that settle in. Then I continued, "You could sum it up this way: your lifestyle is your child's discipleship curriculum."

Blank stares. So, I explained.

"For example, if, to you, following Jesus is nothing more than a hobby to dabble in from time to time, then *that* is what you are discipling your children to imitate. If following Jesus means nothing more than following rules to please others or get approval, then *that* is what you are discipling your children to imitate. If following Jesus means nothing more than dutifully going to church every Sunday, then *that* is what you are discipling your children to imitate. *But...* if following Jesus means joining him on a daily adventure and living a fulfilling life for the good of others, then *that* is what you are discipling your children to imitate."

Silence. But I was starting to see sparks of understanding in their eyes. So, I pressed on.

"The question, then, for you parents is, '*How are you living out your faith*, and *is that what you want your kids to grow up and imitate?*' Because, as the old saying goes, 'What they see is what they'll be.'"

More silence. But I decided they needed what was next, so I leaned in to deliver it.

"Here's the good news, my friends. *You've got this*. You truly do. God has set you up to *succeed* in discipling your own kids.

"Think about it. From the moment your child was first placed in your arms, you've been their hero. God literally wired your child to look up to you and their mom, absorb your examples, and *want* to be just like you. That literally means God designed your child to *want* to be discipled by you – not to be lectured by you, or drilled by you – but to be *shown* by you how to live life well. They *want* you to do that. All you have to do is not screw it up! Don't be a jerk. Don't be self-absorbed. Don't be demeaning. Don't be a religious hypocrite. The bar is really quite low."

I laughed and they nervously chuckled along.

"Instead, as St. Paul reminds us in Galatians 5, all we really have to do is let our family experience the fruit of the Spirit through us: his love, joy, peace, patience, kindness, and self-control. Friends, your families don't need you to be perfect, they just need you to be intentional about letting them experience some of the best of who you are.

"That may not always be easy to do, but it is a simple goal. And as often as we fail our families in this – and we will – then we get to humble ourselves once again, fess up to our failure, and ask them for forgiveness. And when we do that, believe it or not, the respect our family has for us will actually grow even deeper."

I saw a lot of deep thinking going on.

"You don't have to be a theological expert or a perfect rule-keeper to disciple your kids well. All they need is for you to be *intentional* about being the kind of Jesus-follower you want your kids to imitate...because they will imitate you. In fact, they already *are*. Does that make sense?"

There were nods all around the table.

I asked, "Will your kids still fuss and complain and test you?" Everyone laughed, and I laughed with them. "Of course, they will!"

Then I looked each of them in the eye as I said, "But in the end, your lifestyle, values, and character will be what most deeply and permanently imprints your kids because that's how God designed it to work. For better or for worse, they are becoming a version of you. So, why not intentionally choose to make it the better version of you?"

I could see by the look on their faces that understanding was emerging. And just in time. I had a flight to catch.

———————

What about you? As you listened to this conversation, what got your attention? How was Jesus messing with you? As a parent, grandparent, or guardian, what light bulbs went on about discipling a child to be a follower of Jesus? What questions do you still have?

If you want to start being more intentional about being the kind of Jesus-follower you want your child to imitate, then come along with

Susan and me as we unpack the parenting/discipling themes that were introduced in the conversation above.

This is going to be fun!

HERE'S THE POINT

God designed your child to watch you, imitate you, and become a version of you...for better or worse. That's how discipleship works. So, the question for parents is, "How are you living out your faith, and is that what you want your kids to grow up and imitate?" Because, as the old saying goes, "What they see is what they'll be."

SUSAN'S SNIPPETS

Do you like what you see in your "mini-me?" It's never too late to grow in grace.

CHAPTER 2

WHAT DOES IT MEAN TO DISCIPLE MY CHILD?

"Follow my example as I follow the example of Christ."

—Paul, a follower of Jesus, writing in 1 Corinthians 11:1

"What I really lack is to be clear in my mind about what I am to do, not what I am to know."

—Soren Kierkegaard, renowned theologian, when he was 17

So, what does it mean to "disciple" your own child?

Like we pointed out in the first chapter, because of the way God wired the child/parent relationship, you're already doing it.

If you're "raising" your child or "parenting" your child, you're already "discipling" your child.

RAISING MY CHILD = DISCIPLING MY CHILD

The question is what are you raising/discipling your child to be and do? Because the words "disciple" or "discipleship" are not ones we often use outside of religious circles, the definitions have become fuzzy for most people. However, these words have synonyms in our modern conversations that *are* familiar.

For instance, "apprentice," "trainee," and "intern" are all synonyms for the word "disciple." So, when we read in the gospels about "the disciples of Jesus," we are reading about "the trainees of Jesus" or "the apprentices of Jesus." Disciples are people who are being mentored by Jesus to become like him and live like him for the good of others.

Jesus explains it this way, "A student is not above his teacher, but everyone who is fully trained *will be like his teacher*," (Luke 6:40).

DISCIPLE OF JESUS = TRAINEE OF JESUS

The word "discipleship" is often associated with "Christian education." In other words, discipleship = scholarship. However, in the gospels, "discipleship" is more than sitting in a classroom, mastering doctrine, and passing a test. Rather, discipleship is Jesus' training process where people literally follow him around to gain experience, skill, and confidence in living like him for the good of others.

DISCIPLESHIP = JESUS' TRAINING PROCESS

To put this into more familiar parenting language, we could say that Jesus' training process for his followers was a kind of parenting process. To highlight the parallel, we could think of Jesus as "raising his kids [his disciples] to live like him." (Jesus certainly wasn't their biological father, but in John 13:33 he does call his disciples "my children.")

DISCIPLESHIP = JESUS' TRAINING PROCESS = A PARENTING PROCESS

If we then go to the New Testament understanding that discipleship is a parallel to parenting, we start to see a *lot* of applications for the parenting/discipling of our children.

Read the following passages and imagine the disciples are not grown adults but impressionable children:

1. Mark 1:17 (NLT) "Come, follow me, and I will show you how to fish for people."

2. John 13:15 "I have set you an example that you should do as I have done for you."

3. John 13:34 "As I have loved you, so you must love one another."

4. Philippians 4:9 "Whatever you have learned from me or seen in me – put it into practice."

5. 1 Corinthians 11:1 "Follow my example, as I follow the example of Christ."

As you can see, discipling/raising your child is not just about *telling your child* what you believe but *showing your child* what you believe *by how you live*. Our words and what we say we believe are important, but what matters most to our child's spiritual formation is how we live out (or don't live out) what we say we believe.

As the old saying goes, "Actions speak louder than words."

And because of that, Jesus says, "Come, follow me." In other words, "Come with me. Let me show you what my words mean by how I live them out."

HOW I LIVE MY LIFE = HOW I DISCIPLE MY CHILD

"Follow me."   "Follow my example."

"Observe how I live."   "Imitate me."

"Learn from how I do it."   "Consider the outcome of my

"Be like me."   way of life."

See the pattern?

That's what "discipling" your child looks like. God wired your child to observe you, follow you, and want to be like you, for better or worse. That doesn't mean your child will become a *carbon copy* of you but a unique *version* of you. God has given your child his or her own unique talents, challenges, interests, and opportunities (see Psalm 139:13-14 and Jeremiah 29:11). Having said that, how you live out your life and faith is still the pattern and object lesson your child is observing and absorbing as they form their own way of life.

So, why not live the better life? Live the joyful, purposeful, fulfilling life of a Jesus-follower. Why? Because your child is following you.

A few years ago, Mark Baacke, my high school biology teacher, posted the following tribute to his late father on Facebook. I asked him if I could include it for you because he captures the essence of what we are talking about here.

> "Twenty years ago today my dad went home to heaven. He taught me how to play golf, ping pong, baseball and how to make a game out of any situation I faced. He taught me always to do my best even at things I didn't like too much (History, English, washing the car, etc.). When something seemed impossible and I felt like quitting, he would say, 'That's no hill for a climber.' Or when a situation totally sucked or was unfair, he'd tell me, 'Sometimes it goes like that for days, and then it gets worse.' I don't recall him ever telling me to be a teacher, but he was such a good teacher himself that I grew up wanting to do what he did. He was serious about the important things in life, but he would be the first one to laugh when life threw him a curve ball. He had the ability to see right through fake people. I think the little kid in the story about the emperor's new clothes probably grew up to be my dad. He loved his country and made it better by being a good man himself.

"Most importantly, he loved his Lord and Savior, and the more I think about my dad, the more I realize how many times and in how many ways he was letting me see that love in the way he treated people and the way he went through life. Over these past 20 years there are lots of memories and images of my dad that have stayed with me, but one keeps coming up more than most. I'm an eight-year-old kid, and dad is taking me fishing. There are tall weeds between where we parked the car and the pond where we're going to fish. Dad goes ahead of me and I try to follow, but soon he's lost from sight, and I'm surrounded by weeds that are twice as tall as I am. We've done this before, and he's taught me not to panic but just to follow the trail of bent and broken weeds. So that's what I do until I reach the pond and find him smiling back at me because he knows where I'll pop out of the weeds. And so it's been 20 years now that I've been walking through the weeds of life without him, but I've got his trail to follow because he intentionally did things to help me see it, and I firmly believe he was following a trail that Jesus left for him. So, one day I'll pop out of the weeds and Jesus will be waiting for me with Dad right there with Him."

Yep. That's what we're talking about. We live and lead so our children can follow and imitate. That's what it means to "disciple" our children.

HERE'S THE POINT

So, what does it mean to "disciple" your own child? Because of the way God wired the child/parent relationship, you're already doing it. If you are "raising" your child, you are already "discipling" your child. As Jesus shows us in the gospels, discipling/raising your child is not just about *telling your child* what you believe but *showing your child* what you believe *by how you live*. Our words and what we say we believe are important, but what matters most to our child's spiritual formation is how we live out (or don't live out) what we say we believe.

SUSAN'S SNIPPETS

You are God's masterpiece. What kind of beautiful painting do your kids see when they look at you? What do you see when you look at them? Many great master artists had apprentices who reproduced their original paintings so more people could enjoy them. For most eyes, it would be difficult to discern the "copies" from the original. We all need some touch up work now and then. Thank God He is the Master Artist!

CHAPTER 3

PARENTING WITH THE END IN MIND

"It is easier to build strong children than to repair broken men."

—Frederick Douglass

"You can't go back and change the beginning, but you can start where you are and change the ending."

—Unknown

So, as you are leading your children through the tall weeds of this world, where are you heading? And is where you are heading where you want to end up? It's important for you to know because your child is attempting to follow you there.

Mark's dad, from our previous chapter, knew he was heading to the pond to fish with his son. He could see the pond as he made his way through the tall weeds, and his path through the tall weeds eventually led his son to the pond, as well. So, where do you want your path to lead your child?

Answer *that* and you will be able to parent with much more *clarity and intentionality*. Answer *that* and you will be able to wake up every morning *knowing* the kind of life you are aiming to live for the sake of the little one following you through the weeds.

For the sake of such clarity, let's work through two questions:

Where do I want my child to end up? (In other words, what are my parenting goals?)

To lead my child there, how then shall I live?

Once you have crafted answers to these questions, you will be able to lead your child through the tall weeds of daily life with much more clarity and intentionality.

Where do I want my child to end up?

As Susan and I prepared to write this book, we asked parents across the country, "What are your biggest hopes, fears, or questions about raising children to be followers of Jesus in this generation?" Here are some examples of what we heard.

Stephanie: "My greatest fear is that they stray from Christ when they no longer live at home. My greatest hope for them is that relying on Christ becomes as normal as drinking water."

James: "You're touching a raw nerve here. How do we help Christian families like mine raise spiritually healthy and mature kids? Too many of our own become cynical, indifferent, or vulnerable because of church activities which entrap them in perfectionism or shame."

Michael: "A huge fear I have is potentially controlling my child too much and instead of passing on a rich appreciation for the Word and an ongoing relationship with Jesus, I indoctrinate them into a hollow religion of just saying and doing the right things."

Can you relate to any of these parents? How would you answer the question? I can hear the hope, but I can also hear the fear. To be honest, the fear comes from a growing realization that what we are currently doing in our attempt to raise life-long followers of Jesus isn't working.

And here's the thing: It isn't.

For quite some time, the way U.S. Christians and U.S. congregations have been raising our children has not consistently resulted in them becoming life-long followers of Jesus. The statistics are stunning. The number of teens and young adults who walk away from the church and even their faith has been on the rise for decades. Both Lifeway and Barna researchers estimate that between 65-70% of teens leave the church and abandon their faith by their freshman year of college. Every parent thinks their child is among the 30% that would never do that, but in every congregation Susan and I work with, we hear heart-breaking stories from parents and grandparents who have children and grandchildren who are no longer part of the Church.

What we are currently doing is not working well enough. And here's why.

For generations, parents have assumed that they are fulfilling their responsibility to raise Christian children if they have them baptized, take them to worship, and make sure they are participating in whatever Christian education programming the congregation requires. If the child compliantly participated, parents considered it a win.

GOING TO CHURCH + PARTICIPATING IN PROGRAMS
+ GOING TO HEAVEN = THE CHRISTIAN LIFE

The problem?

Many young people compliantly followed their parents and congregations down this path, but then found themselves bored and unconvinced by what was presented as "the Christian life." So, when they left home, they simply dropped out.

"Bored and unconvinced." What do I mean?

When we present the Christian life to our children as consisting of nothing more than attending services, keeping rules, and learning the facts and figures of the faith, we have taken something that is alive and meant to be experienced as a daily adventure with Jesus and reduced it to an abstract concept we simply read about.

Some years ago, Susan and I took our teenage daughter on a trip with us to visit friends in North Carolina. While we were there, our friends took us to the Nantahala Outdoor Center (the NOC). Among the many things offered was whitewater rafting. The pamphlet we read made it sound intensely exciting. Ellen, our daughter, really wanted to go. Susan and I, not so much.

So, we signed up Ellen, and while she went with the guide and other adventurers, Susan and I went with our pamphlet and waited for her to finish. While we waited, we reviewed the pamphlet again. Yep, what we read earlier still sounded pretty exciting. However, by the time we had re-read the pamphlet several more times, most of the excitement had drained away. Frankly, we were getting a little bored with it. Same description. Same ride described. But reading it again and again left us... bored. I started checking my phone, and Susan wandered off to take some pictures.

In the meantime, while we were getting bored re-reading the pamphlet, Ellen was having the time of her life! She wasn't reading a pamphlet *about* whitewater rafting; she was *experiencing* it. Of course, it wasn't the pamphlet's fault Susan and I got bored. The purpose of the pamphlet was to describe the ride, not substitute for it. The purpose of the pamphlet was to give the reader just enough information and motivation to get up and join the fun of actually going on the ride of their life!

And that is the mistake we have been making as Christian parents with the Christian faith. We have substituted reading about following Jesus for the actual experience and excitement of following Jesus.

By pointing this out, I'm certainly not saying there's something wrong with reading Bible stories to our children or having them listen to sermons. There's nothing wrong with this, but there is something missing from it. If all we do is have our children study the same Jesus-stories over and over again, but never go on the ride with him, what do you think will eventually happen?

I was talking with a college student who was getting a degree in Christian education. As part of her training, she had been assigned to teach a Sunday School class with six-year-olds. She was amazed by one little girl, who, no matter what Bible story the lesson was covering, could rattle off all the details of the story before the lesson even began.

Although I was impressed by the six-year-old's sharp mind and her parents' commitment to reading the stories with her, I wanted to make a point with the college student. So, I said, "It's fantastic that a six-year-old has so much Bible knowledge at such a young age, but if mastering the stories is your only goal, can you imagine how utterly bored she will be with Sunday School by the time she gets to sixth grade?"

That's not a criticism. It's not the Bible's fault that children eventually become bored with the same stories. After all, the purpose of reading the Bible is to describe the adventure Jesus is offering, not substitute for it. The purpose of reading the Bible is to give the reader just enough information and inspiration to get up and join the fun of going on the ride of our lives with Jesus!

Think about it for a minute. As you read through the gospels, does anyone following Jesus seem bored? Then how did we make following Jesus so boring?

Simple. We settled for reading about it and discussing it rather than participating in it.

So, you see, it turns out young Christians don't drop out because they are bored with "following Jesus." They haven't even been introduced to it yet. Instead, their parents and church leaders have had them spend their entire childhoods listening to lessons about the ride, filling in workbooks about the ride, and reading and re-reading the pamphlet about the ride. *But no one actually invited them into the raft and went on the ride with them!*

Bored with the ride? They haven't even been in the raft yet! They're not bored with "following Jesus" but with what we have *substituted* for following Jesus.

And, by missing out on their adventures with Jesus, not only are young Christians bored by faith, they are unconvinced by it. They have studied the concepts of the Bible, but they lack experiences that would have convinced them of the reality of what the Bible describes. They remain unconvinced of the gospel's power to transform human lives because they have never seen it happen in someone. No one has shown them how to live an adventurous, redemptive life with Jesus for the good of others. No one has challenged them to go out and give it a run themselves. No one has been willing to regularly sit down with them and, in an unhurried way, talk through their experiences, questions, and doubts. All that's been expected of them since they were little was to memorize, attend, and behave. And they did so compliantly.

Unfortunately, when they are old enough to leave home, their Christian faith is untried, untested, and unconvinced. And, therefore, many are poised to walk away. Is that where you want your child to end up? Bored, unfulfilled, unconvinced, and walking away? Of course, not.

The solution? *Take your child on the ride with Jesus!*

You see, Jesus is on a mission. He was sent by his Father on a grand adventure to redeem and restore all things to his Kingdom. And he invites you and your children to join him on the ride of your lives. Not just to study him and worship him. That's great, but that's not all. He also invites you to actually join him on his adventurous mission.

FOLLOWING JESUS = JOINING JESUS ON HIS MISSION = EXPERIENCING ADVENTURES WITH JESUS

When your children actually get in the raft and go on the ride with Jesus, they'll start seeing things and experiencing things they've only heard about before. They'll have stories of their adventures with him. They'll be able to cite the evidence of Jesus' presence and activity in their lives and the lives of others. They'll have a relationship with him and rely on him more and more as their trusted guide.

And they won't be bored.

If *that's* where you want your child to end up, then it's time to answer our next question: To lead my child there, how then shall I live?

HERE'S THE POINT

Where do you want your child to end up? Bored, unfulfilled, unconvinced, and walking away from Jesus? Or as a convinced, life-long follower of Jesus, living a fruitful and fulfilled life for the good of others? Answer *that* and you will be able to parent with much more *clarity and intentionality*. Answer *that* and you will be able to wake up every morning *knowing* the kind of life you are aiming to live for the sake of the little one following you through the weeds.

SUSAN'S SNIPPETS

The next time we went to the NOC, we all went ziplining together. (Yes, including Greg and me...we learned our lesson!) What an adventure we had! We all had stories of feelings, fears, and fun to share around the table that night. Each day is a zipline adventure with Jesus, full of stories to share. Be sure to share them around your table tonight.

CHAPTER 4

HOW THEN SHALL I LIVE?

"The only thing that counts is faith expressing itself through love."
—Paul in Galatians 5:6

"I've laid down a pattern for you. What I've done, you do."
—Jesus in John 13:15 (The Message)

God designed your child to learn from you how to live life. For better or worse, you are their pattern and object lesson. So, the question for every mom and dad becomes: "How then shall I live?"

God's answer? "Live a life of love," (Ephesians 5:2).

That's the life God wants your child to see you living and grow up imitating: a life of love.

LIVING A LIFE OF LOVE = LIVING THE LIFE OF A JESUS-FOLLOWER

Why love?

E-v-e-r-y-t-h-i-n-g good and healthy in the human heart flows from love being freely received, fully trusted, and freely given to others. It's a beautiful circle of abundance and generosity. Human beings thrive when they live in a relationship of love with God and with one another. Break that cycle of love for a human being, and you break that human being.

Restore that cycle of love for a human being, and you restore that human being.

Living a life of love is what God originally created us for (see Genesis 1 and 2), what was lost in the fall (Genesis 3), and what God has now restored to us through the sacrificial death and resurrection of Jesus, his Son (Colossians 1:19-22).

John, one of the twelve original followers of Jesus, sums it up this way: "Dear friends, let us love one another, *for love comes from God*. Everyone who loves has been born of God and knows God. Whoever does not love does not know God *because God is love. This is how God showed his love among us*: He sent his one and only Son into the world that we might live through him. *This is love*: not that we loved God, but that he loved us and sent his Son as an atoning sacrifice for our sins. Dear friends, *since God so loved us, we also ought to love one another*. No one has ever seen God; but if we love one another, God lives in us and his love is made complete in us... *We love because he first loved us*," (1 John 4:7-12, 19).

Do you see the circle of love and life and abundance God restores? From God, to us, through us, to the people around us...all restored because of the atoning sacrifice of Jesus.

So, living the best life for your child to see simply means living a life of love for the good of others as you join Jesus on his mission. And what does a "life of love" look like? That's simple. It looks like Jesus.

LIVING A LIFE OF LOVE = LIVING LIKE JESUS

Wait.

Doesn't "living like Jesus" sound a bit out of reach? After all, he's the Son of God! He healed the sick, calmed the storm, raised the dead, and saved the world! How can we live like him?

Yes, Jesus is the Son of God, but when he says, "Follow my example"

(John 13:15) or when John says that we "must walk as Jesus did" (1 John 2:6) or when Paul says, "Imitate me as I imitate Christ" (1 Corinthians 11:1), they are not talking about imitating the stuff that requires you to be the Son of God but the stuff that requires you to become like a little child.

Oh.

We are not asked to imitate the spectacular *results* of Jesus' lifestyle, only the simple lifestyle itself. What the Father produces through a life – whether Jesus' or ours – is called "fruit," and the kind of fruit the Father produces through someone – whether spectacular or less so – is up to him alone. In the gospels, the fruit that the Father produces through Jesus often looks more spectacular than what he produces through us. However, the actual *lifestyle* Jesus follows is so simple, even a little child can imitate it.

And what was Jesus' daily lifestyle? He simply trusted the Father like a little child (fully and humbly) and then looked for opportunities to offer the Father's abundant love to others. The opportunities the Father prepared for Jesus were often miracles, deliverances, and resurrections, but the lifestyle *itself* was so simple even we can imitate it. (See John 15:1-8, Matthew 18:4, Matthew 6:33, Ephesians 2:10)

LIVING A LIFE OF LOVE = LIVING LIKE JESUS = LIVING LIKE A LITTLE CHILD

So, again, living the best life for your child to see simply means living a life of love for the good of others as you join Jesus on his mission. We presume it must be more complicated than that because...well, it's always been presented to us as something more complicated than that, right? But look at what the Bible actually says:

> Galatians 5:6 says the only thing that counts is faith expressing itself through love.

John 3:16 says the reason the Father sent His Son is love.

Matthew 22:37-40 says the entire Bible hangs on love.

Galatians 5:22 says the fruit of the Spirit is love.

Romans 13:10 says we fulfill every law when we love.

1 Corinthians 12:31 says the most excellent way is love.

John 13:34-35 says the way people will know we are disciples of Jesus is by how we love.

According to the Bible, God's essence is love; God's motivation is love; God's gift is love; God's expectation of us is to freely receive and freely give love; and the result of love is a redeemed and restored world of...love.

Even something that sounds as complicated as Paul admonishing parents to bring up their children "in the training and instruction of the Lord" (Ephesians 6:4) is not so complicated after all. Why? Because at the heart of "the training and instruction of the Lord" are parents exemplifying a lifestyle of...love.

And what does this kind of "love" look like? Jesus shows us.

Jesus' love isn't the world's kind of love which is only given to the loveable or the deserving. Instead, it is a costly, gritty kind of love that is given to people we consider *un*lovable and *un*deserving, especially when those people are members of our own family:

- Like when siblings are fighting, and one chooses to love back instead of hit back.
- Like when parents are arguing, and one chooses to be humble instead of be right.
- Like when someone in the family hurts the others, but those who have been hurt choose forgiveness and reconciliation instead of revenge and retaliation.
- Like when a neighbor or classmate or fellow employee sins

against us, and we choose to treat them better than they deserve instead of giving them what we think they deserve.

Jesus' love is a self-sacrificial love that looks like self-sacrificing service for the good of others. It is a courageous love that shines most brightly in the midst of anger, argument, hatred, and opposition. It is a pursuing love that redeems and restores the fallen, the broken, and the outcast. In a word, it is *grace*. Grace saves people. It forgives people. It offers a way back for people. It heals people. It reconciles people. It restores people. It is the kind of love that Jesus offers you, and it is the kind of love you can now offer your family and your neighbors.

That's what a life of love looks like. "Freely receive, freely give," (Matthew 10:8). It is an abundant, joyful, self-sacrificing, fruitful, and fulfilling way to live. It is redemptive and restorative. It is the life of a Jesus-follower. It is the best way to live. And it is the life we want to intentionally and consistently exemplify for our children, right?

The trouble, of course, is that on our own, we can't consistently exemplify such a life. In fact, if a life of love starts with us, it doesn't have much of a chance. Our tanks are empty. Our wells are dry. However, the good news is that *we are no longer on our own*. We are now what Paul calls, "In Christ." (In fact, he uses the term 79 times in his letters.) Being "in Christ" means the Spirit of Jesus is literally living inside of us enabling us to consistently live a life of love. How does this happen?

In Romans 6:3-4, Paul explains that it is because we are baptized *into* Christ Jesus. "Or don't you know that all of us who were baptized *into Christ Jesus* were baptized into his death? We were therefore buried with him through baptism into death in order that, just as Christ was raised from the dead through the glory of the Father, *we too may live a new life*." Likewise, in Galatians 3:27 Paul writes, "For all of you who were baptized *into* Christ have clothed yourselves with Christ."

When we are "baptized into Christ Jesus," the Spirit of Christ Jesus literally comes to live inside of us. And that changes both who we are and what we have to offer others. We are no longer on our own, because Christ Jesus is now a part of us too. Baptism isn't simply a religious ritual. In Genesis 2, when God breathed his Spirit into Adam, it wasn't a religious ritual. It was literally the way by which his Spirit came to live inside of Adam, and Adam became a living being. In the same way, when we are baptized *into* Christ Jesus, the Spirit of Christ Jesus literally comes to live inside of us, and we become alive in him.

BEING "IN CHRIST" = BEING BAPTIZED INTO CHRIST JESUS = THE SPIRIT OF CHRIST JESUS COMING INTO US = WE ARE NO LONGER ON OUR OWN! WOOHOO!

Because the Spirit of Christ Jesus now lives in us through baptism, he changes who we are and what we are capable of:

"Therefore, if anyone is in Christ, he is a new creation; the old has gone, the new has come!" 2 Corinthians 5:17

"You were washed, you were sanctified, you were justified in the name of the Lord Jesus Christ and by the Spirit of our God." 1 Corinthians 6:11

"Therefore, there is now no condemnation for those who are in Christ Jesus." Romans 8:1

"So in Christ Jesus you are all children of God through faith, for all of you who were baptized into Christ have clothed yourselves with Christ." Galatians 3:26-27

"I can do all things through Christ who gives me strength."
Philippians 4:13

With the Spirit of Christ Jesus now living in us, we have a *new* identity.
We are beloved children of the heavenly King, forgiven, freed, and made
new! And we also have a new *capability* we didn't have before. We are
now capable of doing *everything the Father gives us to do.* Not anything
we want to do, but everything the Father gives us to do – like consistently
living a life of love as an example for our children:

"...for it is God who works in you to will and to act according to
his purpose." Philippians 2:13

At this point, you might be asking, "So, if Jesus really makes us capable
of it, why do so many of us struggle to be more consistent at living such
a life?"

Good question. It's certainly not because we are lacking the strength
or capability to do it. Remember, we are now "in Christ" and Jesus gives
us both his strength and capability in our baptism. However, to live a
life of love more consistently, Jesus invites us to receive one more thing
from him: his *training.* He wants to train us how to *use* the strength and
capability he has given us.

JESUS OFFERS US NOT ONLY HIS STRENGTH AND CAPABILITY, BUT ALSO HIS TRAINING.

It's like we are little babies who need to learn how to walk. At first it
seems impossible that babies would be able to walk on their own. They
are so wobbly and unsteady. They take one step and then fall down onto
their padded little bottoms. But we parents know what our babies are

capable of, so we keep lifting them back to their feet and encouraging them to give it another try. The babies' confidence grows. Their walking skills improve. And soon they are running around, one step after another. Our babies were born with the *capability* to walk, but they needed mom and dad to train them *how* to walk.

This is how it is with discipling your family, as well. You already have Jesus. You already have his love and power inside you, sealed through baptism. You are already "in Christ." Now all you and your children need is Jesus' consistent training in how to freely receive his love, fully trust his love, and then freely offer his love to those around you as you join him on his mission. The question is how does your family participate in his discipling process?

And that's what we will look at next.

"What is Jesus' discipling process and is there a simple way my family can weave it into our daily lives so we get better at living a life of love and joining Jesus on his mission?"

Let's go find out.

HERE'S THE POINT

God designed your young child to learn from you how to live life. For better or worse, you are their pattern and object lesson. Which begs the question for every mom and dad: "How then shall I live?" God's answer? "Live a life of love," (Ephesians 5:2).

SUSAN'S SNIPPETS

One friend of ours was a large, fun-loving, grace-filled teacher who was adored by all. He carried around a Bible so worn it was held together by paperclips and rubber bands. What do your kids see is the source of your love and grace?

CHAPTER 5

HOW TO JOIN JESUS IN DISCIPLING YOUR FAMILY

"By wisdom a house is built, and through understanding it is established."

—Proverbs 24:3

"You buy a TV and it comes with a 1000-page manual. You go home from the hospital with a newborn baby and there's nothing!"

—Will Smith, in the documentary, *Dads*

We've been checking off our parenting questions:

Where do I want my child to end up?

Imitating Jesus and living an abundant, generous life of love as they join him on his mission.

To lead my child there, how then shall I live?

I will set the example by imitating Jesus myself and living an abundant, generous life of love as I join him on his mission.

Are you ready to tackle the next question?

What is Jesus' discipling process and is there a simple way my family can weave it into our daily lives so we get better at living a life of love and joining Jesus on his mission? In other words, what are we actually supposed to *do*?

Maybe you can relate to Susan and me when we were expecting our first child. We wanted to be as prepared as possible. We took birthing classes with experts. We read books like, *What to Expect When You Are Expecting*. We carefully considered names. We converted a bedroom into a cute nursery. And we had highly trained medical professionals lined up at the hospital.

So, when the big day arrived, we were ready. Susan's bag was packed. The diapers for newborns were purchased. We got to the hospital according to schedule. We used our breathing techniques, we timed contractions, we anticipated each stage of birth. And while it may have taken a steady drip of Pitocin, 27 hours of labor and a C-section, our baby finally arrived!

We were exhausted!

We were elated!

As Susan was taken to the recovery room, I took off to make phone calls. "It's a girl!" I announced with great pride. "8 pounds, 1 ounce. And her name is Amanda Jane."

Later, in the hospital room, the maternity nurses were never far away. If we needed any help or had any questions about what to do, they were right there to tutor us. We were such rookies! But then – suddenly – after only a few days under the tutelage of these wonderful baby-experts, they came to our room, helped us bundle up our newborn child, escorted us to the front door of the hospital, and waved bye-bye to the rookies as we drove off...on our own! I was thinking, "What's happening? Are we ready for this?!"

That's when it hit me: We had been well prepared for *delivering* our baby, but now it was time for us to *raise* our baby. At that point, as we were driving our new family home, if you had asked Susan and me about that third parenting question – "Hey Finkes, what's your plan for discipling your family?" – I know we wouldn't have had a very clear answer. I know we *wanted* our family to follow Jesus, but I also know we didn't really have a plan for what we were actually going to *do*.

Well, that was more than 30 years ago. Since then, Susan and I raised three children into adulthood and walked alongside many other parents as they raised their children too. Collectively, we all stumbled through plenty of mistakes, blind spots, and outright sins. But with all that experience, clarity also emerged.

So, if Susan and I had the opportunity to go back in time and sit down with brand new Daddy-Greg and Mommy-Susan, what would we share with them about discipling their growing family? What would we tell them to *do*?

"Watch how Jesus does it in the gospels and then imitate him."

What does *that* mean?

In the gospels, we can actually watch as Jesus disciples his followers. We can take note of *what* he trains them to do and *how* he trains them to do it. We don't have to figure out a *new* way to disciple our family. We can just imitate *Jesus'* way.

What does Jesus train his followers to do?

To live a life of love as they join him on his mission.

How does Jesus train them to do it?

He focuses on three main **discipling priorities:** True Identity, Increased Capacity, and Growing Ability.

He follows a simple **discipling rhythm** every day: Teach Them, Show Them, Send Them, Circle Up with Them.

We will spend the rest of the book talking about how to apply this with your family, but to get started, let's briefly introduce Jesus' discipling priorities and rhythm.

Jesus' Discipling Priorities

Most Christians have great clarity about how Jesus saves people, namely, through his sacrificial death and resurrection for the forgiveness of sins. But how does Jesus *train* people? To answer that, all we have to do is go back into the gospels where we can literally watch and listen as Jesus goes about the work of discipling his followers.

At first, the experience can seem overwhelming because it looks like Jesus is training them in *so many things*! However, the longer we follow him around in the gospels, the more we start to see three main discipling priorities emerge. What are they?

1. **True Identity**

   Jesus works to convince his followers of *their true identity, value, and purpose* which are redeemed and restored through his death and resurrection. He prioritizes this because the more convinced they become, the more they are set free to live in the abundance of the Father's love without reservation or uncertainty as they join Jesus on his mission.

TRUE IDENTITY = CONVINCED THEY HAVE ALREADY
RECEIVED THE FATHER'S ABUNDANT LOVE

2. **Increased Capacity**

   Jesus works to increase his followers' capacity for *trusting the Father more and humbling themselves faster* so they are willing and ready *to generously offer the Father's love to others.* By knowing how to counter their fear and pride with trust and humility, they will be more willing and ready to generously offer the Father's love to others. He prioritizes this because the more capacity they have for trust, humility and generosity, the more powerfully the Father can work through them as they join Jesus on his mission.

INCREASED CAPACITY = WILLING AND READY TO GENEROUSLY OFFER THE FATHER'S LOVE TO OTHERS

3. Growing Ability

Jesus works to grow his followers' ability to practice the following skills: Seeking the Kingdom, Hearing from Him in the Gospels, Talking with People, Doing Good, and Ministering through Prayer. In our first book, "Joining Jesus on His Mission" we call these the Five Mission Practices. Improving these skills puts his followers into better position to seek, recognize, and respond in love to what the Father is already doing in the lives of people around them. Jesus prioritizes this because the more they improve in practicing these skills, the more confident and effective they will become as they join him on his mission.

GROWING ABILITY = IMPROVING SKILLS FOR OFFERING THE FATHER'S LOVE TO OTHERS

We can illustrate Jesus' discipling priorities this way, starting in the center.

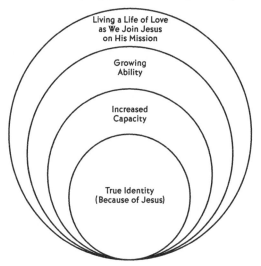

Living a Life of Love as We Join Jesus on His Mission

Growing Ability

Increased Capacity

True Identity (Because of Jesus)

Of course, the discipling priorities we see Jesus focusing on in the gospels are the same ones he invites you and your family to intentionally focus on, as well. We will use the next several chapters to unpack these priorities more thoroughly, but for now ask yourself:

Would you like to see your child convinced of what the Father says is their true identity so they are set free to live in the abundance of his love without reservation or uncertainty?

Would you like to see your child gain increased capacity for godly trust, humility, and generosity so the Father can work through them even more powerfully for the good of others?

Would you like to see your child improving their ability to use the Five Mission Practices so that they grow even more confident and effective at joining Jesus on his mission?

We all would. The only question is *how do we get there*?

This leads us to our second introduction.

Jesus' Discipling Rhythm

In the early chapters of the gospels, the people who started following Jesus are inexperienced rookies. They're not very good at living a life of love or joining Jesus on his mission. In fact, they're a mess. (Like us!) They're uncertain of the Father's love, they're often selfish, and they're usually much more concerned about who is greatest than who needs their love. As such, they aren't much use to Jesus.

However, that's precisely why Jesus is putting them through his training process. He keeps his focus on his discipling priorities (the ones listed above) and then uses his discipleship rhythm to weave his training into their daily lives. What is his weaving rhythm? He keeps it simple:

1. Teach them
2. Show them

3. Send them
4. Circle up with them and share the stories

Pretty straightforward, huh? Jesus teaches them what they need to know, shows them how to put it into practice by how he lives, sends them out to gain their own experience living it, and finally circles up with them to share the stories of what was discovered and learned. Simple but effective.

The result? Over time, day by day, they gained experience and confidence in living a life of love and joining Jesus on his mission...and got *better* at it.

And your family can imitate the same discipling rhythm:

1. Teach them what they need to know.
2. Show them how to put it into practice by how you live.
3. Send them into the day to gain their own experience.
4. Circle up and share the stories of what everyone discovered and learned as they joined Jesus.

By imitating Jesus' discipling rhythm, you are literally joining Jesus in discipling your family. And the more consistently your family participates in his discipling rhythm, the more growth you will see in your family's experience and confidence in living a life of love and joining him on his mission.

Okay, so much for introductions. Now it's time for practical applications. And that's what we will dive into next. But before we do, I have a word of encouragement for you...

You've Got This

If present-day Susan and Greg could sit down with their younger selves, we would tell them one more thing. We would tell them, "You've got this.

You really do. You've got this because Jesus has got you. Yes, keep your eye on the ball. Yes, do your best. But. Here's the bottom line: Jesus has already set you up to succeed in raising your child because he has already given you the most important ingredient for success: Love. And love makes all the difference."

Our baby daughter, Amanda, who I mentioned at the beginning of this chapter, just had a baby son of her own, Emerson Alden. (Yes, we are bursting with pride and joy!) During her pregnancy, her sister Emilie had the fun idea of making a video where family and friends offered Amanda and Kevin (her husband) their best parenting advice. Do you know what the #1 piece of advice was? Whether it was Great-Grandparents, Aunties or young friends chasing around their own toddlers, their advice was the same: The most important thing you can do as a parent is love your little child. Love. Your. Little. Child.

As I write this, there is a popular television series called *This Is Us*. One of the main characters is Randall Pearson, a man who, as an infant, was adopted into the Pearson family after he was abandoned at a fire station. Even though he is deeply loved by his adoptive-parents, Randall has interpreted the act of being abandoned by his birth-parents as a sign that he is unloved. This sense of being unloved and therefore unlovable becomes the core of his life story. It drives him. It binds him. And he can't overcome it. He throws himself into professional achievement, public service, being the perfect son, being the perfect father, and, finally, therapy. But none of it helps. Until...

Until he learns the rest of the story surrounding his birth. Yes, his birth-parents were tragically flawed and, yes, he was left at a fire station. The abandonment was still deeply painful for him. But Randall learns something new about his birth-story and it changes his life. He learns that, despite the facts surrounding his birth, his birth-parents had *loved him after all*. It is so simple, and yet it is a revelation for him. Knowing it changes him. It is like he is able to breathe for the first time. Knowing he is loved means he is able to finally exhale his pain and anger and breathe in the love instead.

After the revelation, there is a poignant scene of him driving home with his wife. She notices there is something "different" about him...that he seems "lighter." And Randall just smiles. He says, "Beth, I know my birth-story...I know my birth-story, and it's not just getting left at a fire station. It's two people, two imperfect people, who loved me."

Randall had a new core for his life story. He was loved after all. And it made all the difference.

And it will make all the difference for your child, as well.

Dear reader, you've got this. No, you won't be the perfect parent, everything won't go according to plan, and you won't raise the perfect child. But parenting-perfection isn't Jesus' goal. Love is. And love will make all the difference as you raise your child. St. Peter once put it this way, "Above all, love each other deeply, because love covers over a multitude of sins," (1 Peter 4:8).

Amen. It sure does. Thanks be to God.

HERE'S THE POINT

When Susan and Greg Finke had their first child many years ago, they were well prepared to *deliver* a baby but not necessarily to *raise* a baby. If they could go back and sit down with their younger selves, what would they share about discipling a growing family? Two words: Imitate Jesus. Imitate both his discipling priorities and his discipling rhythm so that, over time, your family can gain experience and confidence in living a life of love and joining Jesus on his mission...and get *better* at it.

SUSAN'S SNIPPETS

Our family's dinnertime was often the time to share stories. We'd listen, laugh, cry, and ask questions. Greg would then ask, "What do you suppose Jesus was up to in all that?" And we would talk some more.

Our bedtime rhythm included reading stories and praying together. We went through the entire *Chronicles of Narnia* series at least five times! And our girls never got too old for Max Lucado's children's books, *You Are Special* and, *Tell Me the Story* (and neither did we!). Before the girls were old enough to write, I would ask them about their day and write down word-for-word, what they said in a notebook. (Those are precious notebooks now!) We would end with everyone saying a bedtime prayer together and then each person adding their own prayer. (If Emilie was sleepy, she would sometimes just say, "I pray what Amanda prayed.") This bedtime rhythm set groundwork for their personal journaling and prayer time when they were older.

And singing…there was lots of singing in our home! We liked to take Bible passages and set them to melodies that we made up on our own. God wired our brains to better remember when words are put to music! And the girls can still sing those Bible passage songs to this day! Make a joyful noise together!

CHAPTER 6

JESUS' #1 DISCIPLING PRIORITY: TRUE IDENTITY

"How great is the love the Father has lavished on us, that we should be called children of God!
And that is what we are!"

—1 John 3:1

"The truth will set you free."

—Jesus in John 8:32

Because we have the gospel accounts, we can actually watch Jesus as he trains his followers.

We can take note of both *what* Jesus trains his followers to do and *how* he trains them to do it.

What does Jesus train his followers to do?

To live an abundant, generous life of love and join him on his mission.

How does Jesus train them to do it?

He focuses on three main **discipling priorities:** True Identity, Increased Capacity, and Growing Ability

He follows a simple **discipling rhythm** every day: Teach Them, Show Them, Send Them, Circle Up with Them

Because Jesus shows us how to disciple people, we don't have to figure out *new* ways of discipling our family, we can just imitate *Jesus'* way.

And do you know what's really crazy? Imitating Jesus' discipleship process with your family is simpler than you think and a lot more fun! There will be lots of loving and smiling and laughing and joy. There will be lots of creativity and brainstorming as your kids come up with ways to bless people who need a blessing. There will be lots of adventures and excitement and stories. And there will be a growing friendship with Jesus.

It. Will be. A blast!

Parents Go First

When it comes to discipling your family, Jesus invites parents to come along too! In fact, it is crucial that you do. Together, you and your children get to become actual disciples of Jesus and let him show you how to live in the Father's abundant love. Doesn't that sound wonderful? You get to be a fellow-learner with your children and benefit from the experience as much as they do. It will be a family experience!

But your children need you to take the lead and be an example for them. So, you get to go first.

Your children can't follow where you're not leading, and they can't imitate what you're not doing. However, if you start to participate in the Father's abundant love yourself, your children will see how to participate too. Together as a family, you can then help each other learn how to freely receive the Father's love, become fully convinced of the Father's love, and freely offer his love to others.

Where We're Headed

So that we don't get lost in the details, let's look at where we're headed:

- For the rest of this chapter, we will look at why True Identity is Jesus' #1 discipling priority.
- Chapter 7 presents the importance of helping our children connect *knowing* their True Identity in their head with being *convinced of it* in their heart.
- Chapters 8 and 9 walk us through simple tools we can use to disciple our family to live in the power of their True Identity.
- Chapters 10-13 unpack Increased Capacity.
- Chapter 14 focuses on Growing Ability.
- And in chapter 15 we will pull everything together as we focus on Jesus' discipling rhythm.

At first, this may sound like a lot of moving parts, but you'll quickly get the hang of it. How do I know?

Do you remember learning to ride a bike? I do. When my Dad said it was time to take off my training wheels, I thought it sounded like a bad idea. Riding on just *two wheels*? "I can't!" I protested. And I was sure I was right. But Dad gently insisted. As I reluctantly got on, I remember feeling like there was a lot to keep track of: balance, peddling, steering, panic.

I just *knew* I was going to crash! So, I wanted my Dad to hang on to me as I peddled. At first, I was yelling, "Hang on! Hang on! Hang on!" but I quickly switched to, "Let go! Let go! Let go!" because *I started getting the hang of it*. Suddenly, I found myself riding on two wheels and having *fun*! Confidence replaced anxiety and all those moving parts of balance, peddling, and steering came together in one simple motion: riding my bike.

And I haven't felt anxiety about getting on a bike since. Why? Because

I know how to ride now. (Turns out, it's not that complicated after all.)

That's where you're headed with discipling your family too. It's like learning to ride a bike. At first it will seem like a lot of moving parts. But if you keep at it, all those moving parts of Identity, Capacity, Ability, and Rhythm come together in a simple, fulfilling lifestyle. Soon you'll find yourself actually getting the hang of it and having *fun*! So, let's climb on and start our first lesson.

Why is "True Identity" the #1 Discipling Priority of Jesus?

Jesus is on a mission to redeem and restore all things to his Father's Kingdom, and he invites you and your family to join him (Colossians 1:19-20, Matthew 4:19). It is the life you were made for and saved for (Genesis 1:26-28, 2 Corinthians 5:17-21). It is not always the easiest life, but it is a life of abundance, joy, purpose, and adventure (Matthew 16:24-25).

However, for you and your family to be useful to Jesus as you join him on his mission, two things need to happen:

1. Jesus needs to save you from your sins. And there's good news on that front. It is finished! "Here is a trustworthy saying that deserves full acceptance: Christ Jesus came into the world to save sinners – of whom I am the worst," (1 Timothy 1:15).

2. And then Jesus needs to train you to live a life of love so you can *rock* when you join him on his mission. "Follow God's example, therefore, as dearly loved children and live a life of love, just as Christ loved us and gave himself up for us," (Ephesians 5:2).

In the gospels, we see Jesus laying the foundation for living an adventurous life of love by making True Identity his #1 discipling priority. And there's a very good reason why.

From childhood on, every human being has a pressing need to answer three fundamental questions about themselves:

1. Who am I? (What is my true identity?)
2. What do I have to offer? (What is my value to others?)
3. What am I here to do? (What is my meaning and purpose in life?)

These questions sound simple, but they are profound. They are the questions of our identity, value, and purpose. Consciously or unconsciously, every human being wrestles to answer them. And there's a lot riding on *how* people answer them. What people believe about themselves deeply affects their ability to freely receive, fully trust, and freely give away the Father's love...or not.

It works like this: our "identity" is who we believe we truly are. It drives how we evaluate ourselves and whether we believe we have something of true value to offer others. And those two beliefs together drive what we believe is the true meaning and purpose of our lives.

So, what you and your family believe about your true identity literally sets off a chain reaction in your inner being that deeply affects *everything* about you, for better or worse. That's why Jesus makes "True Identity" his #1 discipling priority – a lot is at stake.

For example, if you and your family believe what the Father says is true of your identity, the truth will set you free to live a confident, fulfilling life of love for the good of others. But if you believe what the world, the devil, and even people you trust may say about you, it can lead you to embrace tragically different answers:

1. Who am I? I am a disappointment. I am not enough. I am wrong.
2. What do I have of value to offer others? Nothing. I am worthless. I can't.

3. What is my purpose? I don't know. I have none. I am lost. I may
    as well give up.

If you and your family believe answers like those, it can lead to a
lifetime of anxiety, uncertainty, anger, and despair. And, sadly, that's
where many people find themselves.

The question is why would *anyone* even be *slightly* tempted to
believe such despairing things about him or herself? What is it about
human beings that leaves us believing in our heart of hearts that these
horrible answers might be true? It all goes back to our common history
at the creation of the world. Humanity's true identity – who we were
created to be – was shattered and everyone has been struggling with the
consequences ever since.

Here's what happened: at the creation of the world in Genesis 1 and
2, God formed human beings from the dust of the ground and literally
breathed his life into us so we would become living beings. And along
with his life we received *him*. We received his self-sacrificing love, joy,
peace, goodness, kindness, service, stewardship...and he gave it all to us in
abundance! Along with his abundance, he also gave us a unique purpose
in the created world, namely, to be his physical hands and feet and to use
his abundance for the good of one another. In the beginning, *that's* who
we were created to be and *that's* what we were created to do.

It was our *true* identity, value, and purpose, and it was amazing.

But humanity shattered all that with a deliberate choice that was made
in Genesis 3. It's called *the Fall,* and it was ugly and heartbreaking and
changed everything about us. We chose ourselves over our Father. We
chose our sin over him. We chose a lie over his life and abundance. And
instead of fulfilling our true purpose – tangibly sharing his abundance
with one another – we spread our jealousy, hatred, war, and ruin to
one another. When we rejected the Father's love and abundant life, it

shattered our true identity, value, and purpose. And the horrible answers listed above became true of us instead. We try to deny it, we try to run from it, we try to self-medicate it. But, on our own, we can't *escape* it because, since the Fall, it has been *true*.

Even if someone doesn't know this history, they sense its accuracy. Everyone knows *something* is wrong – that *something* is broken and missing. It's like we understand something was lost because we feel the pain of its absence so strongly.

So, the reason every human being struggles is because we sense the True Identity we lost while still having to bear the shattered identity we are left with.

But. There is also *good news.* "For God so loved the world..."

The good news of God is that, through Jesus' death and resurrection for the forgiveness of our sins, he has reversed the effects of the Fall and has redeemed and restored the *True* Identity, Value and Purpose he intended for us since the creation of the world. "For the Father has rescued us from the dominion of darkness and brought us into the kingdom of the Son he loves, in whom we have redemption, the forgiveness of sins." Colossians 1:14

While the awful answers listed above *used* to be true of us, they no longer are. Through Jesus, we now have a *very different set of answers* we can believe:

Who am I?
I am a beloved child of the heavenly King!

"How great is the love the Father has lavished on us, that we should be called children of God! And that is what we are!" 1 John 3:1

"The Lord your God is with you, he is mighty to save. He will take great delight in you, he will quiet you with his love, he will rejoice over you with singing." Zephaniah 3:17

"Fear not, for I have redeemed you; I have called you by name; you are mine." Isaiah 43:1

> This is who the Father says you are. This is your True Identity.
>
> And you can believe it *without reservation.*

What do I have of value to offer others?
I have the things of the Kingdom in abundance: Love, joy, peace, patience, kindness, grace and truth.

"Have no fear, little flock, for your Father has been pleased to give you the Kingdom." Luke 12:32

"The fruit of the Spirit is love, joy, peace, patience, kindness, goodness, faithfulness and self-control." Galatians 5:22-23

"The greatest of these is love." 1 Corinthians 13:13

> This is what the Father says you have. This is your True Value to others.
>
> And you can believe it *without reservation.*

Think of "the things of the Kingdom" like they are superpowers you and your children can use for the good of other people. In the movies, the superpowers of characters like Wonder Woman and Super Man are make-believe. But the things of the Kingdom are *real.* They are superpowers because they come to us straight from God and have the power to literally change people from the inside out. When we use things like love, joy, and kindness on people, we are literally unleashing God on them!

What is my purpose?
I get to go out every day on mission with Jesus and look for people who need a little of what I already have in abundance and generously offer it to them.

"Come, follow me." Matthew 4:19
"Freely you have received, freely give." Matthew 10:8
"For we are God's workmanship, created in Christ Jesus to do good works, which God prepared in advance for us to do." Ephesians 2:10

This is what the Father says you do. This is your True Purpose.
And you can believe it *without reservation.*

Author Bob Goff has a fun way of describing our True Purpose: "Every day, God invites us on an adventure. It's not a trip where he sends us a rigid itinerary, he simply invites us. And then, leaning over us, he whispers, 'Let's go do that together,'" (from a recent Tweet by Bob Goff).

This is who we are, this is what we have, this is what we do. This is the truth that sets us free. Pretty cool, huh?

And that's why Jesus' #1 discipling priority is convincing us of our True Identity. He knows it is the difference between living with a sense of abundance or scarcity, confidence or anxiety, generosity or selfishness, fruitfulness or despair. When Jesus trains us to become convinced of our True Identity, it sets us free to live in the abundance of the Father's love without reservation or uncertainty. And it sets us free to generously offer his love to others as we join Jesus on his mission.

All we need to do is remember what is true.

Can you imagine being a little child growing up with these truths ringing in your ears and being convinced of them in your heart? That, because of Jesus:

- This is who I am: I am a beloved child of the heavenly King.
- This is what I have of value to offer others: I have the things of the Kingdom and in abundance.
- This is what I do: I go out every day on mission with Jesus and look for people who need a little of what I already have in abundance and generously offer it to them.

Now, let's go see how to make it happen for *your* child.

HERE'S THE POINT

Jesus' #1 discipling priority is training his followers to live in their True Identity. Why? From childhood on, every human being has a pressing need to answer three fundamental questions about themselves:

1. Who am I?
2. What do I have to offer?
3. What am I here to do?

What you and your family believe about your True Identity literally sets off a chain reaction in your inner being that deeply affects *everything* about you. Because of Jesus, you can now answer these questions with the Father's truth. And the truth sets you free to live a confident, fulfilling life of love for the good of others.

SUSAN'S SNIPPETS

In the movie, *A Little Princess*, Sarah tells all the girls that they are princesses. When the mean Miss Minchin refutes that, Sarah cries out, "Yes, they *are* princesses! All girls are princesses! Didn't your father ever tell you that?!" Your kids are princesses and princes of the Most High King! Make sure they hear that from you... often!

CHAPTER 7

TRUE IDENTITY: CONNECTING THE HEAD AND THE HEART

"Jesus loves me, this I know for the Bible tells me so."

—Anna Warner, composer of the song

"God, who is love, still loves. And today his love is experienced in our love."

—John R.W. Stott, Bible scholar

For a very long time, it's eluded us.

As parents, we want our children not only to *know* their True Identity in their head (so they can pass a quiz) but also to be *convinced* of it in their heart (so they are living in its abundance). We want them *to know the truth* that they are beloved children of the heavenly King, but we also want them to *be convinced of the truth* that the heavenly King *truly loves them.*

But how?

How do we make that connection between their head and their heart? How do we turn *knowledge* of what is true into *conviction* of what is true? The answer is to help them experience the very thing they are being told to believe.

HEARING THE TRUTH + EXPERIENCING THE TRUTH = BEING CONVINCED OF THE TRUTH

Where did we get that idea? Jesus. "If you stick with this, living out what I tell you, you are my disciples for sure. Then you will *experience for yourselves* the truth, and the truth will set you free," John 8:31-32. (The Message)

Throughout the gospels, as Jesus trains his followers to live in their True Identity, he works at connecting their *knowledge* of the Father's love with *experiencing* the Father's love to *convince* them that the Father indeed loves them. As Jesus' followers become convinced of the Father's love, it sets them free to live in its abundance without reservation or uncertainty and to freely offer it to others. How does this apply in your family?

The *truth* is that, because you and your family are "in Christ," you are beloved children of the heavenly King. There's really no question about that. But when you *do* question it (and we all do), God invites you to look to the cross. "This is love: not that we loved God, but that he loved us and sent his Son as an atoning sacrifice for our sins," (1 John 4:10).

The proof of God's love is the cross of God's Son. That should settle it, right? "This is most certainly true." However, there is the *truth* that God loves you and then there's the *experience* of God loving you. For human beings to thrive, we need both.

People *experience* God's love through other people. The design is simple: love comes from God *to* us, then *through* us to the people around us (1 John 4:7-12). It is true that we *receive* love directly from God, but it is also true that we *experience* his love through other people. And human beings thrive when we have *both*. Jesus says it plainly, "As I have loved you, now love one another," (see John 13:34).

Children *experience* God's love through their parents. Husbands and wives *experience* God's love through each other. Christians *experience*

God's love through one another in Christian community. Unbelieving neighbors *experience* God's love through Christian neighbors.

So, when your child experiences God's love through you, *the experience becomes the evidence* they need to believe that God indeed loves them too. In other words, their experience convinces them that what they have been told is true. Then, the more convinced your child becomes of God's love, the more they are set free to live in its abundance without reservation or uncertainty and to freely offer it to others.

And your child thrives.

Obviously, a lot is at stake here. So, let's take a little deeper dive.

As we saw in the last chapter, our True Identity as a beloved child of the heavenly King has been redeemed and restored by Jesus. It's done. It's settled. "This is most certainly true."

However, as adults, we also live with the consequences of how well (or poorly) our parents discipled us to live in our True Identity. Do you feel convinced that you are the Father's beloved or are you uncertain? Do you fully trust the Father's love or do you struggle with it? Do you live with a joyful confidence or an anxious doubt?

Of course, we do not rely on our experiences (good or bad) to determine if something God says is true. What is true is determined by what God says, not by our experience. In fact, our faith, by the power of the Holy Spirit, clings to what God says is true *especially* when we aren't experiencing it. However, it is also true that a child's ability to experience and trust God's love is directly connected to how well (or poorly) they experience love through their parents.

As one of my friends once said to me, "I *believe* God loves me. I just have a very hard time *trusting* that." He was raised by parents who were unable to freely express their love to him. His parents were rule-keepers; harsh and disapproving much of the time. The love they did offer him, when it was offered, was conditional. He had to earn it. And then it was quickly withdrawn. He heard about God's love every week in church. He believed the truth of it by faith. (Thank you, Holy Spirit!) However, because of the way he experienced love through his parents, he had a very difficult time trusting that God could love him abundantly and unconditionally.

If you, like my friend, struggle to trust that you are unconditionally loved by God, it may be because of how you experienced love through your parents. If it is easy for you to trust that you are unconditionally loved by God, likewise, it is probably because of how you experienced love through your parents. The *truth* that you are unconditionally loved by God is not affected one bit by how your parents loved you. However, *your ability to understand and trust that truth is.*

Having said that, for those of you who grew up in Christian homes where emotions were suspect or even unwelcomed, reconnecting truth with experience may feel... well, suspect. However, in sending his Son into the world, God himself shows the value he places on reconnecting his truth with our human experience.

For instance, John 1:14 says, "The Word became flesh and made his dwelling among us. We have *seen* his glory... who came from the Father, full of grace and truth." Connecting the Father's grace and truth with our human experience is one of the reasons Jesus came in the flesh. The Father wanted us, his children, who are flesh and blood, to *experience* his grace and truth – to see it, hear it and feel it.

So, he sent his Son to become flesh and blood and live among us:

Touching the leper

Teaching the crowds

Taking children into his arms to bless them

Eating with sinners

Healing eyes and ears and legs
Shedding his blood
Physically rising from the dead

In 1 John 1:1, John unabashedly points to the *tangible experiences* he had with Jesus as the reason he is convinced of the truth about Jesus. "That which was from the beginning, which *we have heard*, which *we have seen with our eyes*, which we have looked at and *our hands have touched* – this we proclaim..."

Jesus came not only to tell the *truth* of the Father's love, but also to help us *experience* the Father's love so that we become *convinced* that the Father really does love us (John 15:9). In other words, Jesus reconnected knowing our True Identity in our head with being convinced of it in our heart by helping us experience it in our daily life.

Why is this so important? Because when we become convinced that the Father really does love us, it sets us free to live in the abundance of his love more fully (John 14:21-23) and to join Jesus on his mission.

BEING CONVINCED OF THE FATHER'S LOVE = BEING
SET FREE TO FULLY LIVE IN ITS ABUNDANCE

Now, how do we as parents do the same thing with our children? How do we actively live in the truth and experience of the Father's love ourselves and disciple (raise) our children to do the same?

Read on, my friend, and in the next chapter Jesus will show us how. (Hint: The answer is simpler than you think and a lot of fun!)

HERE'S THE POINT

The truth is that God loves you and your family. The proof of his love is the cross of his Son. However, there is the *truth* that God loves you and then there's the *experience* of God loving you. For human beings to thrive, we need both. So, when Jesus trains his followers to live in their True Identity, he connects *hearing* the truth of God's love with *experiencing* God's love, so we become *convinced* of his love. And, as parents, we can do the same.

SUSAN'S SNIPPETS

Did you play "Show and Tell" when you were young? Well, we never get too old for "Show and Tell," especially where discipling our kids is concerned. Love is an action. Forgiveness is love in action. Say, "I'm sorry," but then how about showing it too? Words are worthless unless backed up with action. Show and tell God's love daily!

CHAPTER 8

TRUE IDENTITY: PRACTICE REMEMBERING

"Then they remembered Jesus' words."

—Luke 24:8

Our goal is not only to tell our children what is true but also to convince our children of what is true, so they live their life in the abundance of what is true. We want our children *convinced* that Jesus has restored them to being beloved children of the heavenly King, so they *live* as beloved children of the heavenly King...abundantly, freely, generously, and with *real* joy!

Now, how do we get there? Jesus shows us in the gospels:

He practices remembering what his Father says is his True Identity.

He experiences the Father's love as a daily reality.

His daily experience of the Father's love further convinces him of it, so he fully trusts it and is able to offer it generously to others.

He disciples his followers to do the same.

REMEMBERING + EXPERIENCING = CONVINCED + GENEROUS

So, the key to discipling your family to live in their True Identity is following Jesus' example of remembering *and* experiencing the Father's love as a daily reality. It's simpler than you think and a lot of fun! Here's what to do.

How to Help Your Family Remember Their True Identity

At his baptism, the Father declares what Jesus' True Identity is, "This is my beloved Son with whom I am well pleased," Matthew 3:17 (ESV). Even before Jesus has done anything or earned anything, the Father pours out his unconditional love and approval on him. The Father does this so Jesus can live his life and do his work out of the abundance and strength of his True Identity.

And the same is true for you and your children.

Like Jesus, at baptism, the Father declared what your family's True Identity is: beloved children with whom he is well pleased. When each of you were "baptized into Christ Jesus" (Romans 6:3), the Father poured out his unconditional love and approval on you even before you could do anything or earn anything. And the Father did this so each of you can now live your lives and do your work out of the abundance and strength of your True Identity.

Isn't that cool?

Then, after Jesus' baptism, we see why it was so important for him to *remember* what his Father said about his True Identity: first the devil, then the crowds, and even his own family and disciples aggressively tempt Jesus to abandon his True Identity for a false one (see Matthew 4:1-11, John 6:26, Mark 3:21 and Matthew 16:22). Jesus has to diligently practice remembering his True Identity in order to resist the temptations, stay on course, and remain fully fueled for pursuing his True Purpose, day after day. And the same is true for you and your children.

The devil aggressively tempts your family to abandon your True Identity for a false one. He wants you feeling confused, worthless, and empty so you use up your life pursuing everything *but* your true purpose. Don't be naïve or unaware. The devil knows what's at stake. And so should you and your family.

The devil is fully aware that your abundant strength is rooted in your True Identity as a beloved child of the heavenly King. He knows that the more deeply you are convinced of your True Identity, then the more abundantly, confidently, and purposefully you and your children will be able to live. So, the devil tempts you to believe your identity comes from *anything* besides that truth. He wants you to believe your identity is rooted in your failures, your lack of achievement, your outward appearance, your quirks, your inability to measure up, the opinions of others.

A lot is at stake. That's why 1 Peter 5:9 says, "Resist the devil." How? By "...standing firm in the faith." In other words, the way you resist the devil's lies is by standing firmly on what the Father has already said is true about you.

One of my children likes to journal as she reads her Bible and prays. So, every Christmas and birthday she puts journals on her gift list. Last year I gave her one that had this printed on its cover: "Whenever you feel overwhelmed, remember whose daughter you are and straighten your crown." I love that! When you remember who you truly are, it sets you free to live in that truth, straighten your crown, and reject the ridiculous lies of the devil.

In fact, Jesus has that very thing in mind when he says, "The thief comes only to steal and kill and destroy. I came that they may have life and have it *abundantly*," John 10:10 (ESV). Did you hear that? Jesus came so you can live in abundance not scarcity, confidence not anxiety, generosity not selfishness, fruitfulness not despair. He's already brought all this to you! You don't have to chase after it or go earn it. All you have to do is remember that you already have it!

Make sense?

So, diligently practice remembering. When your family follows Jesus' example, you too will be able to stay on course and remain fully fueled for pursuing your True Purpose, day after day.

Simple Ways to Practice Remembering

One way to "practice remembering" is for your family to speak to each other what the Father says is true:

> This is who we are: beloved children of the heavenly King!
>
> This is what we have to offer: the things of the Kingdom and in abundance!
>
> This is what we do: we go out with Jesus and look for people who need a little of what we already have in abundance and generously offer it to them!

Think of it as your family's cheer and creed: "This is what we believe!" Having a cheer-creed is a simple way for your family to help each other remember your True Identity, Value, and Purpose every day.

Even if your child is an infant, you can "practice remembering" with them. Look your sweetie in the eyes, hold their little hands, and speak into them what the Father says is true, "This is who you are. This is what you have. This is your true purpose in the world." You get to be the reason your little child grows up with the truth of the Father ringing in their ears each day.

If your family is a little older, imagine huddling at the front door every morning like a team getting ready to take the court or the field. Everyone's hands are extended into the middle, and, on the count of three, everyone calls out the family's cheer-creed! By reminding each other of what the Father says is true, you can head out the door with clarity and courage for another day of adventuring with Jesus!

BECAUSE OF JESUS, THIS IS WHO WE ARE! THIS IS WHAT WE HAVE! THIS IS WHAT WE DO! WOOHOO!

Of course, if your family's personality is a little less boisterous, you can do the same thing using fewer exclamation points.

No matter what cheer-creed you choose, the key is to use one. Practice it together. Recite it together. Shout it together. Whisper it together. Have fun with it together. But use it.

Use it to...
Cheer each other on
Pick each other up
Remind each other
Challenge each other
Correct each other

And use it a lot. Because, as you know, the temptation to give up and disbelieve what your Father says is your True Identity is relentless.

There are many other ways to help your children practice remembering:

Remind them of who they are and what they have as superpowers from God. Superpowers = the things of the Kingdom they have received from God like love, joy, peace, and kindness. Then encourage them to use those powers on people during the day. As you have opportunity, watch your children and take note of when you see them use their superpowers. Later, as you Circle Up to tell the stories (there will be much more on "Circling Up" in chapter 15), you can remind them of what you saw. "When I saw you do _____, *that's* what Jesus is talking about in the Bible." This reinforces their understanding of what it means to live in their True Identity by connecting their experiences during the day with what the Bible says.

Have your children write down who they used their superpowers on during the day (or, if they are small, you can write it down for them). Then, when you see a difference in the person's life, you can remember what was offered and give thanks to God for what he did through those simple actions.

You can do something similar with your children's prayer requests. Keep a record of who and what they prayed for in the name of Jesus so that, when the Father responds, together you can remember and give thanks.

Speaking of prayer, I used prayer every morning to help my daughter Ellen practice remembering her True Identity before heading into her day. We had a rule that no one left the house in the morning, no matter how rushed or late they might be, without the benefit of prayer. To do that, I basically turned our family cheer-creed into a brief prayer. It reminded Ellen of who she truly was (a beloved, forgiven child of the King), what she had of value to offer others (the things of his Kingdom in abundance), and what she was now heading out to do with Jesus (look for people who needed a little of what she already had in abundance).

The prayer reminded her, empowered her, and focused her for the adventures with Jesus that lay ahead.

When reading the Bible together (or a Bible Story Book), you can point out passages that talk about your children's True Identity, Value, or Purpose. For instance, when you're reading about Jesus' followers, you can remind your children, "That's who *you* are too! You are a disciple of Jesus just like they are." Or when you're reading about God's love, joy, and peace, you can remind them, "That's what *you* have too! It's one of your superpowers from God." Or when you're reading about offering people grace and forgiveness or doing good for them, you can remind your children, "That's how *you* join Jesus on his mission too." Again, this helps your children connect what you are reading in the Bible with their experiences in daily life and reinforces their memories of what it is like to live in their True Identity for the good of others.

To help remember Bible verses that are especially meaningful to your family, you can pair the verses with fun little tunes you make up. Music has an amazing way of helping cement things into our memories. (Think of advertising jingles you can't get out of your head.) Susan did this with our children as they were growing up. She had special Bible verses she wanted to use when our kids were afraid or needed encouragement or needed a laugh. To this day, if one of us starts singing one of those little ditties, the rest of the family can quickly join in! What's a fun little tune you can pair with verses about your family's True Identity, Value, or Purpose? Maybe 1 John 3:1, or 1 John 4:7, or 1 John 4:19?

What are other ideas you have for helping your family practice remembering their True Identity?

Next up, how to disciple your family to live in their True Identity by helping them experience the Father's love as a daily reality.

HERE'S THE POINT

In the gospels, Jesus shows us how to disciple our family to live in their True Identity. The first step is to practice remembering. Your family can follow Jesus' example by speaking to each other about what the Father already says is true of you. By speaking what is true, you are reminding each other of what is true so you can head out the door with clarity and courage for another day of adventuring with Jesus.

SUSAN'S SNIPPETS

When our oldest daughter first started sleeping in her own bed in her own room, sometimes she was a little concerned about what might be lurking in the dark. We didn't want to use pretend "monster spray." Instead, we taught her to say, "Go away, monsters! I'm baptized!" We wanted her to know her true identity and her true source of courage. She made quite an impression on a babysitter one night!

CHAPTER 9

TRUE IDENTITY: EXPERIENCING THE FATHER'S LOVE AS A DAILY REALITY

"And Jesus took the children in his arms and blessed them."

—Mark 10:16

*"When we are filled with the love of God,
the first place for it to be manifested is to our family.
Until our family sees what we are talking about,
they will never hear our words.
We have to act God's love."*

—Corrie Ten Boom

I remember it because of how it made me feel.

Snuggling up with my mom as she read me a story. My dad taking my hand as we walked from our blue van into the school. My uncle complimenting me for being observant. My dad and grandpa including me when they played golf even though I was only seven years old. My aunts being interested in what I had to say.

All this happened more than 50 years ago. Simple little demonstrations of their love. But so important for little Greg. You see, what human beings feel in our hearts is what we remember in our heads. And what I felt in those little moments of demonstrated love was this: I was valued by my family.

And the more I *felt* valued, the more convinced I became that I *had* value. I was told many times a day that I was loved, and that was important. But I *knew* I was loved because my family also demonstrated their love and made me feel valued.

EXPERIENCING LOVE = FEELING VALUED

All this combined to steadily lay a foundation of unconditional love on which little Greg could build his life and faith. "Life *and* faith?" Yes, because when children experience their family's love, it convinces them that God really could love them too. And that's what happened for me. There was never one big event that convinced me of my True Identity as a beloved child of the heavenly King. Rather, I simply grew up experiencing love and feeling valued by my family so that little by little, day by day, it was an easy step to believe that the Father called me his beloved too.

And the same is true for your child. When your child experiences your love, they feel valued. And that combination steadily lays a solid foundation of love on which they can build their life and faith. When they grow up experiencing your love and feeling valued, it is a much easier step to believe that, because of Jesus, the Father calls them his beloved too.

Sadly, as simple as that is, such intentional demonstrations of love don't happen as often as parents might assume or as their children need. Days are busy, schedules are hurried, and parents are distracted.

As a young Daddy, I learned this lesson the hard way. I was sitting with little Emilie on my lap. She was chattering away about something she thought worth communicating to me. To be honest, I was distracted and not really paying attention to her. My eyes (and my attention) were on the newspaper I was reading. I thought I could get away with it by at least *pretending* to listen while my eyes continued to read. Well, little Emilie was having none of it.

She put her hands on my cheeks, turned my head to hers and said, "*Daddy*. Listen to me with your *eyes*."

It was just a moment in time; just one missed opportunity to show my love and help her feel valued. But over time, too many missed opportunities would weaken her foundation. I'm not sure I had all that figured out yet, but, by God's grace, I sensed it was time to set my paper aside and listen to Emilie with my eyes. Instead of a missed opportunity, Emilie felt valued – and her foundation, instead of being weakened, was further reinforced.

In the gospels, Jesus shows us how important this really is. In fact, it is a key part of how Jesus trains his followers to live in their True Identity.

How so?

As we watch Jesus in the gospels, we see him not only teaching people the truth of the Father's unconditional love, but also demonstrating that love in a variety of ways so people could *experience* it as something tangible and real – something they could see, feel, and fully trust (see John 15:9-12).

He defended the woman caught in adultery, he hugged little children, he ate dinner with Zacchaeus, he willingly went to the cross. Jesus demonstrated the Father's unconditional love by loving people in ways that could be *experienced*. And by experiencing Jesus' love, people felt valued and became convinced that the Father really could love them too.

And he wants us to do the same in our family.

Like Jesus, we not only want to teach our children the truth of the Father's unconditional love, but demonstrate that love in a variety of ways so they can *experience* it as something tangible and real. For better or worse, our children experience the Father's love most tangibly through us, and that experience deeply affects their ability to understand and trust his love as they grow into adulthood.

If we demonstrate a kind of love that is conditional and unreliable, our children will grow up struggling to trust that the Father's love could be anything different. On the other hand, if we are intentional and consistent in demonstrating unconditional love to them, they will grow up convinced that their heavenly Father could love them unconditionally too.

Some parents worry they are failing to lay a solid foundation of love for their children because they sometimes blow it. However, raising children who are convinced of the Father's love is not a result of perfect parents loving their children perfectly. When we blow it with our children (and we often will), the key is admitting it and apologizing. If we refuse to do this, we will eventually raise children who resent us and struggle to trust God. But, if we humble ourselves, confess our wrong, and ask their forgiveness, love will prevail. And the Father's kind of love will be reinforced after all.

Again, I learned this lesson the hard way as a young Daddy. I don't remember what little Amanda did, but it was some minor disobedience to which I responded with way too much anger. I was an idiot. I made my little girl cry and sent her to her room with an angry shout. Susan, my wife, witnessed the whole thing and was having none of it. (You can probably guess who Emilie got that from.)

Susan quietly but firmly told me I was wrong for how I handled the situation and that I should go to Amanda and apologize. At first, I stubbornly defended myself and refused to confess. After all, I am the Dad and she is four years old. Dads don't apologize to four-year-olds...do they?

But it was no good. As I reflected, I realized Susan was right and I was wrong. And worse, I realized I had made Amanda feel like I did not value her. Call it what it is: I sinned against Amanda. So, I reluctantly went to her room, explained that Daddy was wrong for what I had done, apologized, and asked her if she could forgive me. I felt embarrassed. I felt foolish. But do you know what I learned? Humbling myself, confessing my obvious wrong, and asking to be forgiven made Amanda feel valued again.

If we humble ourselves, confess our wrong, and ask forgiveness, love prevails and the Father's foundation of love is reinforced after all.

Simple Ways for Parents to Demonstrate the Father's Love

As you think of ways to demonstrate love to your children, keep it simple. Your children need less of the spectacular and more of you.

Whenever you pour a little of yourself into your children – your attention, your interest, your smile, your respect, your time – you are demonstrating your love and their value. And, as you pour, you are reinforcing their True Identity as beloved children of the heavenly King.

Which of the following do you think would help your child feel most loved and valued by you?

- Seeing on your face that you enjoy being with them
- Laughing at their jokes
- Hugging, snuggling, or holding their hand
- Listening with your eyes
- Being interested in their opinion and asking more questions
- Giving them specific compliments about specific actions or characteristics
- Putting your phone down and making them your priority
- Expressing your pride in their best efforts (especially when they fall short)

- Inviting them to come along with you as you run an errand, go on a walk, or work on a project
- Making sure they know they have your love apart from any performance, achievement, or failure
- Confessing when you have wronged them and asking for forgiveness
- And, of course, letting them hear you say, "I love you!" several times a day

One of my children felt loved and valued when her opinion was sought. For another child, it was when I laughed at her jokes and complimented her cleverness. For another, it was big hugs and unhurried snuggles.

If you are unsure of what will make your child feel particularly loved and valued, ask them. Even asking will make them feel loved and valued!

Bottom line? Whatever makes your child feel loved and valued, be intentional about doing it often. Little by little, experience by experience, you are helping your child lay a solid foundation of love on which they will build their lives, their sense of identity, and their faith.

———————

One more thing, and it's important...

For some of you, demonstrating unconditional love to your child comes easily and naturally. In fact, you're already doing it often. And nothing gives you more joy.

But for some of you, demonstrating such love to your child is neither easy nor natural. Perhaps when you were a child, your parents withheld demonstrations of love from you. Perhaps they were preoccupied or just didn't know how. Perhaps there was mental illness or emotional woundedness or addiction.

Whatever the reason, you may be the latest in a long line of family members who did not experience unconditional love as a child. And now that you are a parent yourself, you struggle to freely offer such love to your own child.

You're not to blame for it, of course. You grew up with an unstable foundation; you were never shown how to live in the abundance of the Father's love; you were raised to have deep reservations about your value and worth; and even though you know good and well what the Bible teaches about God's love, you still struggle and often believe the devil's lie that it couldn't possibly be true for you.

You're not to blame for any of it, but you are in danger of passing this legacy on to your child.

Is there hope?

Well, of course there is hope because there is Jesus. Remember what we said about the truth being true whether you experienced it or not? The proof of God's love is the cross of God's Son. However, we thrive when we have *both* the truth of God's love *and* the experience of God loving us.

So, here's the important thing I want you to know: the *experience* of that love, which was withheld from you by your parents, *Jesus has already restored to you*. The *experience* of God's love is not just your gift for someday in heaven but for each day – and abundantly. Now, how can you start *experiencing* for yourself the abundant love the Father already has for you and which Jesus has already restored to you?

It may sound counter-intuitive, but because God already lives in you, you can start experiencing his love by taking action with his love, even if you don't yet feel his love.

C.S. Lewis put it this way, "Do not waste time bothering whether you 'love' someone; act as if you did. As soon as you do this, you find one of the great secrets. When you are behaving as if you loved someone, you will presently come to love him." The reason this works is because it is how God designed love to work. 1 John 4:12 says, "No one has ever seen God;

but if we love one another [action verb], God lives in us and his love is made complete in us [that is, "full, abundant, overflowing"]." What John is saying is that as you put God's love into action for your child (even if you don't yet feel the love), the love of God that is within you starts to flow through you and you begin to feel its abundance yourself. "And his love is made complete in us."

Works every time.

Here's how to get started:

> "Practice remembering." Remind yourself of what is true, "This is who I am: I am a beloved child of the heavenly King. This is what I have: I have his love in abundance!"

> Next, whether it feels natural to you or not, plan a small demonstration of your love for your child.

> Make it something simple that will make him or her feel valued. (Use the list above to spark ideas.)

> Then do that for your child once a day, every day, for three weeks. And smile as you do it.

Think of this like it's as a daily prescription you are taking to help you and your child feel better. Again, it may sound counter-intuitive, but because God already lives in you, you can start experiencing his love by taking action with his love, even if you don't yet feel his love. And within a few weeks, both you and your child will be experiencing the Father's abundant love in your inner being.

HERE'S THE POINT

As parents, we want our children growing up with both the *truth* of the Father's love ringing in their ears and the *experience* of the Father's love as part of their daily reality. When you are helping your children remember and experience the Father's love, you are discipling them to become convinced of their True Identity and to live in it.

SUSAN'S SNIPPETS

As busy, fulltime ministry parents, we needed to be intentional about expressing love in tangible ways. One of the fun ways we did this was to make a list with the girls at the beginning of each season (winter, spring, summer, and fall) of what they wanted to do as a family. Then, we made sure to follow through by planning their requests into our schedule.

Interestingly, the lists were never filled with extravagant, expensive things; but rather they were filled with family time together: picnics in the park, bike rides, swimming, trips to the Whippy Dip for an ice cream cone, going to the farmers' market, apple-picking, backyard camping with s'mores, making snowmen, caroling, ice skating on our frozen mini-pond, family game nights in front of the fireplace...these were the activities our kids prioritized for us. We also had fun going on "adventures" where we piled into the minivan but didn't know for sure where we would end up or what we would see. The girls felt valued and loved because we asked their input and followed through...and together we made wonderful family memories and traditions.

CHAPTER 10

INCREASED CAPACITY: JESUS' NEXT LEVEL OF TRAINING

"Freely you have received, freely give."

—Matthew 10:8

Discipling our children to live a life of love has two parts: freely *receiving* the Father's abundant love and then freely *offering* it to others.

So far, we have been focusing on how to disciple our children to freely receive the Father's love. Now we want to see how we can join Jesus as he increases our children's capacity for freely offering the Father's love to others. This next level of training includes increasing our children's capacity for the following:

Trusting the Father more
Humbling themselves faster
Offering love to others more courageously and generously

The more capacity for these traits Jesus builds into our children (and us!), the more our family will thrive and the more useful we will be as we join Jesus on his mission. Which brings us to one of the more ironic things Jesus requires of his trainees in the gospels: to grow up and become like little children.

In Matthew 18:2-4, the disciples had once again been arguing among themselves about who was greatest. (In fact, this was becoming a habit). So, Jesus sits down and asks a little child to come to him. Taking the child in his arms, he says point-blank, "I tell you the truth, unless you change and become like little children, you will never enter the Kingdom of Heaven. Therefore, whoever humbles himself like this child is the greatest in the Kingdom of Heaven," (see also Mark 9:35-36).

So, to become "great" a person needs to become like a little child? When you think about it, Jesus is making a lot of sense.

He's pointing out something which is obvious even if it is often overlooked: Little children begin life possessing a tremendous capacity for spiritual traits like love, trust, humility, and generosity – the very traits through which the Father can work most powerfully for the good of others. Sadly, it is as little children "grow up" and become more "adult-like," that they start to lose those capacities. Instead, they start to become consumed with questions like, "Who is the greatest?" And, frankly, once a person gets to that point, the Father still loves them, but they aren't of much use to him.

> AFRAID, FULL OF THEMSELVES & SELFISH =
> NOT MUCH USE TO THE FATHER
>
> TRUSTING, HUMBLE & GENEROUS =
> GREATEST USE TO THE FATHER

So, Jesus tells his trainees that they need to change and become like little children again: full of trust, humility, and generosity. However, he doesn't sit around waiting for his trainees to randomly regain those child-like capacities on their own. Instead, throughout the gospels, we see Jesus actively engaging them in his next level of training.

Why focus on trust, humility, and generosity? Because when Jesus' trainees trust the Father more and are able to get over themselves faster, they experience a remarkable increase in their willingness to be generous with the Father's love. And being generous with the Father's love is how they join Jesus on his mission and fulfill their true purpose. The Father has already given them the things of his Kingdom and *in abundance*! However, their capacity to offer that abundance to others generously and courageously is severely reduced by their fear, pride, and selfishness. It's like their child-like capacities became corroded and clogged as they grew up.

That's why Jesus engages them in his next level of training. He needs to clear out their clogs and restore their capacities. And Jesus is doing the same thing with our families.

Max Lucado once put it this way, "Jesus loves you just the way you are but he loves you too much to leave you that way!" Jesus' deep love for your family is revealed not only in how he redeems and restores you but also in how he trains you to overcome your fear, pride, and selfishness so you *can* live generously and courageously for the good of others. And who wouldn't want that for their family?

But it will require Jesus' next level of training to get there.

And there's something you need to know up front about Jesus' next level of training: it's not easy. Like any "next-level" of training, it gets harder on the trainees. It has to. The only way to build more trust in the Father is by facing scarier things that require more trust. The only way to build more humility is by repeatedly coming to the end of ourselves in deeper humility.

So, as counterintuitive as it may seem, when you encourage your children to do hard or scary things with Jesus for the good of others, those experiences actually accelerate their spiritual growth and increase their child-like capacities. Of course, as a parent, our natural instinct is to *protect* our children from hard, scary experiences, not encourage them! Even Mary the mother of Jesus wanted to protect Jesus from hard, scary things (see Matthew 2:14-15, Luke 2:48, Mark 3:20-21). However, courage doesn't increase by playing it safe, and trust in the Father doesn't increase by choosing the easy way.

I ran across a post attributed to a youth pastor which sums up well the tension parents feel:

"Don't be afraid for your kids because the world they are growing up in is not what it used to be. God created them and called them for this exact moment. Raise them up to know the power they walk in as children of God. Train them in the authority of His Word. Teach them to walk in faith knowing that God is trustworthy. Don't teach them to be fearful and disheartened by the state of the world but hopeful that they can do something about it. God knew Daniel could handle the lion's den. He knew David could handle Goliath. He knew Esther could handle Haman. He knew Peter could handle persecution. He knows that your child can handle whatever challenge they face in their life. Don't be scared for your children, but be honored that God chose you to parent the generation that is facing the biggest challenges of our lifetime. Rise up to the challenge. Raise Esthers, Daniels and Davids! God isn't scratching His head wondering what He's going to do with this mess of a world. He has an army He's raising up to drive back the darkness and make Him known all over the earth. Don't let your fear steal the greatness God placed on them. I know it's hard to imagine them as anything besides our sweet little babies, and we just want to protect them from anything that could ever be hard on them, but they were born for such a time as this."

—Alex Cravens

"Don't let your fear steal the greatness God placed on them." Wow. So, again, as counterintuitive as it seems, encourage your children to do hard, scary things with Jesus. It's how he trains them to face their fears and overcome their pride. It's how he makes them stronger, wiser, and more confident. It's how he clears out their clogs and increases their capacity for trust, courage, humility, and generosity – the very traits through which the Father can work most powerfully for the good of others as they join Jesus on his mission.

How do I know?

Look at what the Father was able to do through the courage, humility, and generosity of people in the Bible like Joseph, Elizabeth and Barnabas; Mary Magdalene, Peter and John; Lydia, Paul and John the Baptist. They stood up to the powerful; they stood with the outcast and the poor; they stepped in to care, serve, and restore. They did the right things and the hard things and the scary things that needed to be done for the good of other people. And when they were little children, they all were in the care of their parents.

What do you think their parents were like? I imagine they were a lot like us, trying their best to find a balance between protecting their children from real danger while raising them to be courageous boys and girls of God. Whatever we may think, we know what Jesus thinks. "Let the little children come to me and do not hinder them, for the Kingdom of God belongs to such as these," (Mark 10:14). Jesus wants us to let our children come to him so he can love them and bless them, yes, but also so he can train them to fulfill their purpose as they join him on his mission.

In the next three chapters, we will look at what we can do to join Jesus in discipling our children to fulfil their purpose by trusting the Father more, humbling themselves faster, and offering courageous love more generously. However, you better buckle up first. Turns out, becoming like little children is more exciting than you might expect. Just ask Peter and his buddies.

HERE'S THE POINT

Discipling our children to live a life of love has two parts: freely *receiving* the Father's abundant love and then freely *offering* it to others. So far, we have been focusing on how to disciple our children to freely receive the Father's love. Now we want to see how we can join Jesus as he increases our children's capacity for freely offering the Father's love to others. This next level of training includes increasing our children's capacity for the following:

Trusting the Father more
Humbling themselves faster
Offering love to others more courageously and generously

The more capacity for these traits Jesus builds into our children (and us!), the more our family will thrive and the more useful we will be as we join Jesus on his mission.

SUSAN'S SNIPPETS

"Don't let your fear steal the greatness God has placed on them." Wow! This mom needs to hear those words repeated often. One of our daughters recently shared that her college friends were surprised we let her participate in things their parents were afraid to let them do: such as a summer-long mission trip in Taiwan, a total immersion language program in China the next summer, living among refugees in Fort Worth during the height of the COVID pandemic, etc.

She thought we were being strong, courageous, and fearless the whole time. How wrong was she! I told her, "I was super scared! But I knew you were praying and following God's lead and we needed to do that too."

I had to trust the Father and be humble so she could love others more courageously and generously.

Sometimes the hardest, scariest, most courageous thing we do as parents is to let our kids do hard, scary, courageous things. It just might be Jesus' next level of training for us too!

CHAPTER 11

TRUSTING THE FATHER MORE: RAISING COURAGEOUS BOYS AND GIRLS OF GOD

"Safe? Who said anything about safe? Of course, he isn't safe.
But he's good."

—Mr. Beaver speaking about Aslan the King,

The Lion, The Witch and the Wardrobe

It was a scary, dramatic moment.

But, then again, it needed to be for Jesus to make his point.

Joining Jesus on his mission requires great courage. And Jesus knows the best way to build it in his trainees is not just to *discuss* it but also to be in situations that *require* it. And while this approach can be hard on them, he knows it will be worth it. Jesus has his eye on the prize: The more his trainees come to trust the Father's love, timing, provision, and purposes, the more the Father will be able to use them as they join Jesus on his mission.

So, he goes to work on them.

They are all in a boat crossing the Sea of Galilee, and Jesus is taking a nap (see Matthew 8:23-27). At some point, a "furious storm" blows in and waves start crashing over the boat with such force that the trainees are afraid they will drown. They cry out to Jesus who finally wakes up. And *while the storm is still raging around them*, he says, "You of little faith, why are you so afraid?"

Are you kidding me? Waves are *literally* overwhelming them, and Jesus uses it *as a training opportunity*? Yep. In fact, when you are a follower of Jesus, *every* hard, scary experience is really a training opportunity.

HARD, SCARY EXPERIENCES = TRAINING
OPPORTUNITIES WITH JESUS

You see, that's how Jesus builds their capacity for trusting the Father more: by having them face scary things that require more courage. It's hard on them, but it's the only way. So, while the storm still rages and the danger is still real, Jesus stamps the moment with his question: "Why are you so afraid?"

The trainees: "Why? How about the storm? How about the waves? How about we're going to drown?"

Jesus: "How about you think the storm has more control over you than the Father does? My friends, your fear doesn't come from the storm; it comes from your lack of trust in the Father. That's why you are so afraid. Trust the Father more and you will have more courage as you face scary things like storms."

Ah. Point made.

Jesus then gets up, and says to the raging waves, "Quiet. Be still." And immediately it becomes completely calm. Jesus is showing them in real time that "trusting the Father more" results in more courage. He doesn't settle for having his trainees simply *discuss* the concepts of trust and courage; he looks for experiences that actually *build* trust and courage in them. Experiences are definitely harder on them than discussions, but experience is the only way to actually increase their capacity for trust in the Father and courage in their hearts.

And Jesus wants parents to join him in doing the same for our children. We can intentionally use moments when they are feeling fear to help them build more trust in the Father. More trust in the Father results in more courage for them to face scary things.

MORE TRUST IN THE FATHER = MORE COURAGE
TO FACE SCARY THINGS

If we understand this, we can help our children embrace any hard or scary thing that happens in their daily lives for what it really is: a training opportunity with Jesus. Instead of an experience overwhelming our kids, we can help them lean into how Jesus is going to use it to help them increase their capacity for trust and courage.

Of course, courageously facing scary things with Jesus is different than courageously doing stupid things on our own. When I was about ten years old, I was playing "army" with my friend Duncan. I had climbed on the roof of our house in a move meant to outsmart him. However, Duncan discovered me up there and threw a hand grenade at me. (Don't worry, it was only a pinecone.) To avoid the hand grenade, I courageously jumped off the roof. Regrettably, I landed on a root and turned my ankle so badly I limped for two weeks.

Compare my story of "courage" with my daughter Amanda's story.

When she was eight years old, Amanda, Susan, and I were on the U.S.-Mexico border. The three of us were part of a mission team heading into Mexico the next morning. We had been delayed by a little trouble at the border and had to spend the night on the U.S. side. By now it was nighttime and Susan and Amanda were walking across the compound to where we would be sleeping. Holding Amanda's hand, Susan was thinking to herself, "What have I done bringing my little girl into this?" Almost as if Amanda was reading her mind, she looked up at Susan and said, "Mommy, I'm scared, but I know God wants me to be here."

Would it have been safer for Amanda if we had not brought her along? Maybe. But by including her, she learned how to intentionally put more trust in the Father and take courage in the face of something scary. No amount of abstract discussion could have produced the level of real trust and courage she gained through this one experience. The experience was definitely harder on her than a discussion, but her experience was much more effective at increasing her capacity for real trust and courage.

And the storm of Matthew 8 did the same thing for Peter and his buddies. However, Jesus was not done with them yet. Not even close. He wanted to increase their capacity for trusting the Father *even more*. And Jesus wants the same for us and our children. He knows that the more we come to trust the Father's love, timing, provision, and purposes, the more the Father will be able to do through us as we join Jesus on his redemptive mission.

How do I know? Because it's what we see Jesus doing in the gospels with his original trainees over and over again. Jesus keeps looking for moments when they are feeling fear to help them build *even more* trust in the Father.

For instance, fast forward several weeks from Matthew 8 to Matthew 14:22-33 where we find Jesus using *another* scary, dramatic experience as a training opportunity.

And, by the way, keep your eye on Peter this time. He's starting to catch on.

Again, the trainees are in a boat on the lake. It's about 3:00 a.m. Again, the wind is whipping, the waves are churning, and most of the men are crying out in terror. But not Peter. Peter is standing with one foot on the siderail of the boat ready to step out! *Why?* Because Jesus is standing on the water several paces beyond the boat *inviting him to come*!

What is going on?

Jesus is using another scary experience to press his trainees into trusting the Father *even more*. And Peter seems to be ready. It's as if he is remembering the other storm and how Jesus challenged them with his question, "You of little faith, why are you so afraid?"

So, with his foot on the siderail and courage in his heart, Peter calls out, "Lord, if it's you, tell me to come to you on the water." I can imagine Jesus smiling with pride as he says, "Come." Peter then steps out of the boat and starts walking on the water towards Jesus. Look how much Peter's trust and courage has increased since Matthew 8!

However, Peter is still a trainee, and he makes a trainee mistake. He takes his eyes off Jesus. It's just for a second, but it's enough. In that second, Peter sees the waves, becomes afraid, loses his trust, and begins to sink. He cries out to Jesus, who immediately reaches out his hand and catches him. Of course.

But then listen closely to what Jesus says to Peter next, "You of little faith, why did you doubt?" This isn't Jesus scolding Peter. This is Jesus *coaching* Peter. In fact, I can imagine the conversation going something like this:

Jesus: "Catch your breath, my friend. Now, think about it. What caused your faith to shrink? Why did you doubt?"

Peter: "Why did I doubt? Because I took my eyes off you and let the waves undercut my trust in the Father, that's why."

Jesus: "Good call. Now, draw from this experience the next time you face something that requires you to trust the Father more... because, Peter, there will be a 'next time.'"

Note that Jesus doesn't kick Peter out of his training program because he "failed." In fact, when someone is a trainee of Jesus, failure isn't failure anymore. It's training. Jesus uses Peter's "failure" to build his capacity for trusting the Father *even more* the next time.

FAILURE = TRAINING = INCREASING OUR CAPACITY FOR TRUSTING THE FATHER EVEN MORE

Jesus could have used Peter's failure to crush him or coach him. Since Jesus had his eye on the prize, the choice was simple. He knew that the more Peter and his buddies trusted the Father's love, timing, provision, and purposes, the more the Father would be able to do through them as they joined Jesus on his redemptive mission. So, he used their failures not to crush, but to coach.

We can apply Jesus' wisdom with our children as well. We can help our children change their "failing stories" into "training stories" by asking questions like the following:

What did you learn?

What were you afraid of?

Why did you doubt?

What did you find out about yourself?

What did you find out about the Father?

Now that you've been through this experience, what can you do differently next time?

There would be many more scary experiences for Peter and his buddies in the time they had left with Jesus. And they would often fail. But Jesus kept at it. He kept using their moments of failure as training opportunities (see Matthew 16:13-17:12, Matthew 17:14-21 and Matthew 26:36-75.) And look at the results. By the time we see our friends in the Book of Acts, they have become bold, confident, and courageous. Jesus' next level of training was more "exciting" than any of them could have imagined. But it worked. Jesus grew them up to become like little children again. And Jesus invites you to join him in doing the same for your family.

Simple Ways to Help Your Family Trust the Father More

Sometimes people ask, "What is the difference between trust and faith?" Of course, in many ways, trust and faith are synonymous. However, I find it helpful to make this distinction: faith is given, trust is built. Faith is a gift given to us by the Holy Spirit (Ephesians 2:8-9), whereas trust is built as we go through scary or hard experiences which require us to put more trust in the Father (2 Corinthians 4:16-17).

Of course, the Father is utterly trustworthy from the start. Unfortunately, the only way for us to discover that for ourselves is through experiencing hard, scary things. So, how can we help our children build trust and gain this invaluable experience?

Baby steps.

"Scary" is in the eye of the beholder, right? The disciples were scared by the storm. Jesus was not. Jesus was already convinced of the Father's trustworthiness. The disciples were still learning. Therefore, Jesus regularly used what the disciples *thought* were scary situations to help them take baby steps into trusting the Father more. We can follow that example when our children are feeling fear too.

For instance, when Emilie was about two or three, our family was in a hotel swimming pool. Amanda was older and having fun jumping off the edge of the pool over and over again. I asked little Emilie if she wanted to do that too. She said "no" because she was scared of going underwater. I saw an opportunity for her to take a baby step toward more trust and courage. So, I said I would catch her when she jumped in.

She reluctantly agreed, and I lifted her up to the side of the pool. She stood there dripping FOREVER. She would inch her way forward but then hesitate and move back. Again, and again. I knew I would be trustworthy in catching her, but she still had to find that out for herself. And there was only one way for little Emilie to do that: the hard way. She had to summon more courage and trust her Daddy.

And eventually she did. She held her nose, took courage, and jumped in! As promised, I caught her so her head wouldn't go underwater. She giggled with excitement. "I want to do it again, Daddy!" And that's how we spent the rest of our time in the pool, jumping into the water over and over again. She had to learn the hard way that she could trust me to catch her. But she did. And the more she trusted me, the more courage she had for taking the next leap!

Learning to overcome fear on the side of the pool was just a baby step for Emilie. But baby steps add up. Over the years, her scary experiences helped her understand how to trust her heavenly Father more and more. The more experiences Emilie faced, the more experience she gained. She is now a young woman and she knows how to face scary things with trust in the Father and courage in her heart.

When Ellen, our youngest daughter, was about five years old, our family was driving cross-country to visit relatives. We stopped for a break at a park where there happened to be a live oak tree with long, sweeping branches. One of the branches swept close enough to the ground that Ellen thought it would be fun to climb on it. So, she asked me to lift her up. After she was up there, though, she suddenly felt fear. "Get me down, Daddy. I'm afraid I'll fall!" I was still holding her hand, and I knew there was nothing to fear. But "scary" is in the eye of the beholder, and from Ellen's perspective this was scary. So, I took the opportunity to help her gain a little experience with taking courage.

As she sat on the branch, we talked about what it means to take courage. We talked about how being brave doesn't mean we don't feel fear, it just means we don't let our fear stop us. So, I invited Ellen to do that – to take courage and climb across the branch even though she still felt afraid. And she did! When she got to the other side, she was so proud of herself. She had a big smile on her face. "I did it, Daddy!" "Yes, you did, Ellen! You were brave."

It was just a baby step, but baby steps add up. After that, whenever little Ellen was afraid, I would remind her of what happened when she took courage on the tree branch. Throughout her school years, we would intentionally use the scary experiences she faced to help her understand how to trust her heavenly Father more and more. The more experiences Ellen faced, the more experience she gained. Whether it was starting middle school, having a difficult conversation with a friend, getting on a plane to study Mandarin in China, serving in a refugee community during the COVID pandemic, or sharing the gospel with college classmates, each experience increased her capacity for trusting the Father more – his love, timing, provision, and purposes.

Those baby steps add up. And as parents, we can watch for them and use them.

Perhaps Amanda was so brave on the U.S. border because of an experience she had when she was even younger. She was maybe three years old. She was lying in her bed trying to go to sleep. But she was scared.

"What are you afraid of, sweetie?"

"Monsters."

Hmm… I tried logic with her: "There's no such thing as Monsters."

That didn't work. I tried a parenting tip I had read about in an article. I took a can of air freshener and sprayed it under her bed. "This is a spray that gets rid of Monsters."

That didn't work either. Her fear returned as soon as I walked out of the room. Finally, it occurred to me that I was leaving her helpless in the face of her fear. Instead of Daddy denying Monsters or spraying them, I needed to give her a way to deal with them herself.

So, I simply told her the truth.

"When the Monsters scare you, remember who you are. You are a baptized child of God. That means you have Jesus in your heart and Monsters have to go away if you tell them to. So, the next time you are afraid of the Monsters, you tell them, 'Go away, Monsters. I'm baptized.' Can you do that? Let's practice." We practiced saying it together a couple times, prayed a little prayer, and I left the room.

Sure enough, just a few minutes after I left, I heard Amanda telling the Monsters to go away and with surprising authority! And they must have because Amanda was soon asleep. She was able to overcome her fear because we showed her how to trust her heavenly Father and take courage with authority.

A few weeks later, Susan and I hired a babysitter so we could have an evening out. When we got home, the sitter was wondering what was going on. "I heard Amanda say, 'Go away, Monsters. I'm baptized.' But when I went in to check on her, she was sound asleep." Yep. That's what happens when little children receive Jesus' next level of training.

It was only a baby step, but those baby steps add up. By the time Amanda was going to college in Chicago, she was leading groups of students into the city to serve among the homeless. By the time she graduated and moved to Houston, she rented a garage apartment in an urban neighborhood so she could love and serve that community up close. Where did she find the courage to do all that? It had been building for years – baby step by baby step.

It's not that the Finke sisters are fearless; they are just experienced. Every time they trusted the Father and took courage, they discovered that they could trust his love, timing, provision, and purposes *even more*. Whenever they faced a new challenge, Susan and I could remind them, "Hey, you've seen this before. You have experience with this. What did you do the last time? How did your heavenly Father prove trustworthy?"

The same is true for your children. A little boy who learns how to trust the Father and take courage as he faces little challenges, grows up to become a man who knows how to trust the Father and take courage as he faces big challenges. A little girl who learns how to trust the Father and take courage as she faces little challenges, grows up to become a woman who knows how to trust the Father and take courage as she faces big challenges.

Here are some other ways Susan and I intentionally helped our children build trust in the Father and take courage:

> **We embraced the truth that what they see is what they'll be.** So, Susan and I did our best to set an example of trust and courage for our children. We often talked with them about the scary things we were facing as adults and how we chose to trust the Father more and take courage as we faced them. We tried to set the example that trust and courage was a first response not a last resort.
>
> **Whenever one of our children was in the middle of their own challenge (small or large), we would encourage them to watch how the Father would again prove himself trustworthy with his love, timing, provision, and purposes.** As they wove their way through their uncertain times, we would point to new developments and say, "See? That was God." (see Luke 16:10)

Prayer was at the center of these conversations. We would talk together about what was happening and then talk with God about it in prayer. Susan and I would keep track of what the children prayed so we could help them recognize when God acted (see Luke 11:1, 13).

We encouraged them to pay attention to the little blessings that happened around them. Instead of crediting "luck," we would say things like, "Did you see that? That was God coming through for you again." We wanted our children to recognize what was really happening behind the scenes: that the Father was being faithful. (see James 1:17)

We had a family attitude that was shaped by verses like Romans 8:28 and 31-32. "And we know that in all things God works for the good of those who love him, who have been called according to his purpose... What, then, shall we say in response to this? If God is for us, who can be against us? He who did not spare his own Son, but gave him up for us all – how will he not also, along with him, graciously give us all things?"

At bedtime, we read books like The Chronicles of Narnia about the stories of children who went on adventures with Aslan the lion (who is a Jesus-figure in the stories). These adventures required courage of the children and built their trust in the Father. We would then talk about how following Jesus isn't necessarily safe either, and how it often requires us to be brave as we face scary things for the good of others.

Finally, as they grew, we let them do hard, scary things with Jesus for the good of others. Naturally, our preference as parents was to have our children avoid such things. But we knew the only way for them to learn to live an abundant, fruitful life of love was to let them go on hard, scary adventures with Jesus.

For instance, adventures like having friends who didn't share our faith; going to serve the poor, the homeless, and the oppressed; going on mission trips to places like Mexico, Guatemala, Haiti, Taiwan, and Ghana; heading out on their own to places like China, Australia, Chicago, Austin, Knoxville...you get the idea. These adventures required not only great trust and courage of our children but also of us as their parents. We wanted to keep them safe, however, we knew we needed to let them go with Jesus for their next level of training. And the more experiences they had with him, the more experienced they became in trusting the Father more and living a courageous, generous life of love.

We didn't always do this perfectly, but we tried to do it intentionally. Playing everything safe sounds good on the face of it. But safety isn't really the goal, is it? Living a courageous, generous life of love is. It is the way of a Jesus-follower. It is the most joyful, fruitful, and fulfilling way to live. It is not safe, but it is very, very good. And if we want our family to get there, we will want to join Jesus in doing hard, scary things for the good of others.

It's hard, but it works.

HERE'S THE POINT

Joining Jesus on his mission requires great courage. And Jesus knows the best way to increase courage in his trainees is not just to *discuss* it but to be in situations that *require* it. And while this approach can be hard on them, he knows it will be worth it. Jesus has his eye on the prize: the more his trainees come to trust the Father's love, timing, provision, and purposes, the more the Father will be able to use them as they join Jesus on his mission. And Jesus wants us to join him in doing the same thing for our children.

SUSAN'S SNIPPETS

Our girls had a sign hanging in their bathroom as a daily reminder of why they could take courage: "All I have seen teaches me to trust the Creator for all I have not seen," Emerson.

CHAPTER 12

HUMBLING THEMSELVES FASTER: RAISING HUMBLE CHILDREN WHO ARE FULL OF CONFIDENCE

"In his pride, the arrogant does not seek him; in all his thoughts there is no room for God."

—Psalm 10:4

"God has given each of you a gift from his great variety of spiritual gifts. Use them well to serve one another."

—1 Peter 4:10 (NLT)

Remember our cheer-creed?

- **This is our true identity:** we are beloved children of the heavenly King!
- **This is what we have to offer:** the things of the Kingdom and in abundance! (love, joy, peace, patience, kindness, grace, and truth)
- **This is our true purpose:** we join Jesus on his mission, looking for people who need a little of what we already have in abundance and generously offer it to them!

It's a pretty cool way to live as a family, right?

There's only one problem: us.

The Father has already redeemed and restored us through the death and resurrection of Jesus and given us the abundance of his Kingdom. But our willingness to generously offer that abundance to others can be severely reduced by our fear, insecurity, arrogance, or selfishness. In other words, by us.

Of course, Jesus knows this. So, as we watch him throughout the gospels taking his followers through their next level of training, we see that as much as he focuses on training them to "trust the Father more," he also puts a premium on training them to "humble themselves faster."

Why humility too? When our family learns to humble ourselves and to do it faster, we experience a remarkable increase in our willingness and readiness to generously offer the Father's abundance to others.

HUMBLING OURSELVES = INCREASED WILLINGNESS
AND READINESS TO GENEROUSLY OFFER THE
FATHER'S ABUNDANCE TO OTHERS

AND HUMBLING OURSELVES FASTER = US OFFERING
THE FATHER'S ABUNDANCE SOONER

What do I mean by "willingness and readiness?" As the cheer-creed reminds us, each day when our family wakes up, we have one true purpose: in the midst of everything going on around us, we are to be the ones who join Jesus and look for the people who need a little of what we have already received in abundance from the Father – love, joy, peace, patience, kindness, grace, and truth. Ephesians 2:10 says that the Father prepares such people and opportunities in advance for us.

That means the Father has already woven a plan and timing into our days. There's what we have planned, and then there's what he has planned. There's our schedule, and then there's his schedule. So, we bring a simple discipline into our days: When we see the people the Father has prepared in advance for us, we are willing and ready to humbly set aside our plan and schedule so we can respond to the Father's opportunity (which is going to be more interesting and redemptive than whatever we had planned anyway). And the *faster* we can humble ourselves, the more immediately we will be able to respond in the Father's moment of opportunity, rather than ignoring it because we have our own priorities.

This is the discipline Jesus himself shows us in the gospels. When the Father brings someone across his path who needs a little of what he already has, Jesus doesn't ignore, hesitate, or procrastinate. He doesn't negotiate – "Hey Father, how about we do this later, say tomorrow or next Thursday?" No, Jesus humbles himself quickly – in the moment of opportunity – and steps in. He explains it like this, "...for I seek not to please myself but him who sent me," (John 5:30).

As Jesus' trainees, all we have to do is imitate his simple discipline, right? Unfortunately, on our own, we don't want to.

We forget our days are not our own, that it's not about us, that there's a *reason* the Father has given us his abundance. We have our own priorities and to-do lists. We have our own insecurities and excuses. We have lots of reasons to hesitate, procrastinate, and negotiate when the moment to offer love arrives.

To put it bluntly, we are full of ourselves. It was true of the original disciples, and it is true of us. And there's not much the Father can do through us for the good of others when we are full of ourselves:

I'm too important to help.

I have more pressing things to do.

I shouldn't have to be inconvenienced.

I have my rights.

I should get my way.

Such arrogance, whether found in ourselves or in our children, shuts us off from God and other people. It's easy to see how arrogance weakens and hinders us, and why Jesus needs to train it out of us if we are going to be useful to him on his mission. According to Jesus, the remedy is humility.

Remember Matthew 18:4? "Therefore, whoever humbles himself like this child is the greatest in the kingdom of heaven." But what exactly is humility? I have found that it's easy to spot but harder to define. Whenever you see people doing the following, you are looking at humility in action:

- Collaborating and cooperating instead of trying to dominate and get their own way
- Being quick to listen, slow to speak and slow to become angry instead of insisting they are right
- Admitting their wrongs and asking for forgiveness, as well as freely forgiving those who have wronged them
- Being the peacemaker rather than escalating the argument
- Living with a sense of gratitude and contentment rather than entitlement and greed
- Being able to laugh at themselves and not take themselves too seriously
- Seeking and honoring the insight, input, and help of others
- Having an easy willingness to share, serve, listen, learn, and include
- Having patience, flexibility, and compassion
- Being polite, respecting elders, letting others go first, and being willing to compromise
- Being able to freely offer grace rather than seeking to get even

Like I said, humility is easy to spot. People with such qualities stand out. But it's harder to define the actual humility that produces such qualities.

For instance, when we open a dictionary, it defines humility by what it is *not*. It says something like, "Humility is not being arrogant, proud or haughty." I get that. That's helpful. Kind of. But Jesus tells us to have the discipline to proactively humble ourselves like a child. So, when the dictionary simply defines humility as "a lack of arrogance," it doesn't really help us understand what humility *is* or what we are supposed to *do*. "Not being arrogant" certainly is a first step, but then what?

Let's have Jesus teach us, so we can then teach our children:

1. For Jesus, humility is an attitude that starts with how we see ourselves before the Father and then affects how we treat the people around us (John 1:14, Philippians 2:4-11, John 4:34).

2. There are two parts to humbling ourselves:
   Setting aside our egos (Matthew 5:3, Matthew 16:24, Matthew 23:12).
   Trusting the Father more than we trust ourselves (Matthew 5:1-10, Luke 22:42).

3. Humility produces two practical results in our family which makes us more useful to Jesus as we join him on his mission:
   Being willing and ready to stop and respond when we see the opportunities the Father has prepared for us (John 4:35, Matthew 20:25-28, Matthew 20:29-32).
   Perhaps surprisingly, becoming more *confident* (John 5:20, John 14:12-14, John 15:5). Wait. Jesus wants us to become more *confident*? Yep, stay tuned.

4. Humility is a discipline Jesus develops in his trainees that we can become better at (Mark 9:35, Matthew 18:1-4, Luke 18:9-14).

With that in mind, here's a stab at a definition: "humility" is the habit of looking at the Father and myself and then having the good sense to set myself aside and trust him more than I trust myself.

HUMILITY = SETTING MYSELF ASIDE AND TRUSTING THE FATHER MORE THAN I TRUST MYSELF

Humility is not so much about me being useless, feeling worthless, and lacking confidence as it is about being trained to set my ego aside and put my confidence in the *Right Person* (see Philippians 4:13). It isn't anti-confidence, it is anti-arrogance and anti-worthlessness. Humility is not so much about my *inability* as it is about trusting the Father's *greater* ability.

When I have the good sense to do that, there is more room in my head and heart to willingly and quickly respond to what the Father has prepared in advance for me. This is what John the Baptist is getting at in John 3:30, "He must become greater; I must become less." This is what Jesus is getting at in Matthew 5:3 "With less of you there is more of God and his rule." (The Message)

LESS OF MY EGO = MORE ROOM FOR RESPONDING TO WHAT THE FATHER HAS PREPARED

So, when the Bible says things like, "Humble yourselves under God's mighty hand," (1 Peter 5:6), and "Do not think of yourself more highly than you ought," (Romans 12:3), it isn't promoting my guilt, shame, or worthlessness. It's actually amazingly good advice:

The Father is able to do all things, and I am not.

His wisdom and understanding are complete, and mine are not.

His love is an everlasting love, and mine is not.

He has a redemptive plan which includes every person everywhere, and I do not.

When I look at the Father's abilities compared to my own, the choice is a no-brainer. It's just plain smart to set my ego aside in favor of the Father's mighty hand. It's just plain smart to pray, "Not my will, but yours be done," (Luke 22:42). It's just plain smart to head into the day trusting his timing, ability, and plan more than my own. And the more experience we and our children gain with this, the more confident we become, not in ourselves but in him.

And that brings us back to the surprising topic of confidence. When you first saw the title of this chapter, "Raising Humble Children Who Are Full of Confidence," you might have thought it was a paradox. After all, are Christians even allowed to be confident? But the title is not a paradox; it's what happens when our children learn to humble themselves and put their full trust in *the Right Person* (God).

For example, look at the trainees of Jesus in the gospels. At first, they kept making the same rookie mistake: putting their confidence in the *wrong persons*, namely themselves – who was better, who was greater, who was more deserving. They were confident alright. Confident in their own superiority. And, sure enough, their arrogance was their downfall time and again. They misunderstood, misjudged, misfired, and sunk. They underestimated some things and over-thought others. They denied, doubted, and deserted. It could have left them feeling worthless, useless, and disqualified. But Jesus steadily trained it out of them. And by the time we see them in the Book of Acts, they are living with confidence because they have finally learned to trust the *Right Person* (God) more than themselves.

HUMBLY TRUSTING THE RIGHT PERSON =
GREATER CONFIDENCE

Having said that, humility is not only the remedy for our arrogance, but, perhaps unexpectedly, it is also the remedy for our feelings of worthlessness, uselessness, and insecurity. We probably get how humility is the remedy for arrogance, but for feelings of worthlessness too? Yep. Here's why.

It's easy to see that arrogance weakens and hinders us. But so does a sense of worthlessness. Both attitudes clog us up for responding to the opportunities the Father has prepared for us to do. Arrogance keeps us from *wanting* to. Feelings of worthlessness keep us from believing we *can*. However, both those who are arrogant and those who feel worthless have made the same rookie mistake: they have put their confidence in the *wrong* person...namely, themselves.

Jesus offers a better way: the remedy of humility. He invites us to look at the Father and ourselves realistically and then simply to have the good sense to set ourselves aside (both our arrogance and our insecurity) and to trust him more than we trust ourselves. With full confidence in the *Right Person* (God), we can be like the little children Jesus points to in Matthew 18 – humbly seeking and responding to the opportunities before us with carefree and confident hearts.

So, that's why Jesus wants parents to raise our children (disciple them) to "trust the Father more" and "humble themselves faster." It is his goal for them to grow up to be both humble *and* confident as they join him on his mission in their daily lives.

Unfortunately, the only way for our family to learn humility is the hard way. And it's almost always painful. Humility is certainly important to teach, but it's also tricky to get right. Let's take a deep breath, turn to the next chapter, and then dive into the model Jesus has already shown us.

HERE'S THE POINT

In the gospels, Jesus trains his followers not only to "trust the Father more," but also to "humble themselves faster." When our family learns to set aside our egos and to do it faster, we experience a remarkable increase in our willingness and readiness to generously offer the Father's abundance to others. And, perhaps surprisingly, *the way* Jesus trains his followers in humility actually results in them becoming *more* confident. Jesus would have us raise our children in the same way.

SUSAN'S SNIPPETS

Wow! This is a hard one! Notice we don't have family stories shared here...maybe because the ones that come to mind would need to be in a long chapter called, "Arrogance and Pride Displayed Too Quickly: Raising Kids to Be Like Jesus Not Like Us!" Thank You, Lord, that you are a God of grace and "start overs."

CHAPTER 13

THE TRICKY BALANCE OF RAISING CHILDREN TO BE HUMBLE

"'God opposes the proud but gives grace to the humble.'
Humble yourselves, therefore, under God's mighty hand,
that he may lift you up in due time. Cast all your anxiety
on him because he cares for you."

1 Peter 5:5-7

In Matthew 5:3 we hear Jesus say these words, "You're blessed when you're at the end of your rope. With less of you there is more of God and his Kingdom." (The Message)

At first, this teaching sounds pretty awesome, doesn't it? Who doesn't want more of God and his Kingdom in their life or the life of their children? However, having to come to the end of our respective ropes to *make* that "room" doesn't sound quite so awesome.

What Jesus is describing here is *how* we learn humility. And, unfortunately, the only way for us and our children to learn it is the hard way: by experiencing the pain of coming to the end of ourselves and having our egos deflated. However, this pain has a payoff. Less ego means more room for God and his Kingdom in our lives. Less selfishness, arrogance, and indifference means more room in us to receive God's abundance and more readiness to offer that abundance to others around us.

Humility is the remedy. However, *the process* for learning such humility is usually painful. No child *likes* being humbled by a parent. And that's what makes training our children to be humble so tricky. We don't want to raise our children to become arrogant and full of themselves; but we also don't want to over-correct and raise them to be insecure and feeling worthless either.

It's a tricky balance to get right:

Opposing their arrogance while building up their confidence

Correcting them with the law while affirming them with the gospel

Decreasing the size of their ego while increasing the room they have for experiencing God in their lives

Because every child and every situation is unique, getting the balance right is more an art than it is a science. In fact, Martin Luther once wrote, "Hence, whoever knows well this art of distinguishing between Law and Gospel, him place at the head and call him a doctor of Holy Scripture."

Wow. In other words, it's a tricky balance to get right. However, let not your heart be troubled! The good news is that in the gospels Jesus shows us a simple framework for how he goes about training his followers to be humble – a framework parents can follow as we seek to train our children to be humble too.

So, what do we see in the gospels?

Jesus practices humility *himself.*

He is clear about *what* he is doing as he trains his followers.

He is clear about *why* he is doing it.

He loves his trainees enough to *keep at it.*

First, Jesus practices humility himself: he understands that his trainees will be influenced by what he *does,* not just by what he *says*. In other words, "What they see is what they'll be." Therefore, every day, Jesus shows his trainees how to humble themselves under the Father's mighty hand by practicing it himself. For Jesus, it's not just a lesson, it's a lifestyle.

Next, Jesus is clear about *what* he is doing: he understands that teaching humility involves a measure of pain for his disciples. Yes, the disciples' big, proud, selfish egos only get in their way. Yes, they will have so much more room for God and his Kingdom in their lives as Jesus helps them learn to get over themselves faster. But Jesus never loses sight of the fact that *what* they are experiencing is painful. And because it is painful, he is careful.

Jesus is also clear about *why* he is doing it: the pain of learning humility has a payoff. When Jesus deflates, corrects, or humbles his disciples, it is not a release for his anger or frustration. It is because of his great love for them and for the sake of humility's payoff: having more room to receive God's abundance and more readiness to offer that abundance to others around them.

Finally, Jesus loves his trainees enough to *keep at it*. Training someone to become humble doesn't happen in a day, but rather day after day. Like we said, it's not a lesson, it's a lifestyle. Training his followers requires attention, intentionality, and consistency day after day. And, he loves them enough to keep at it.

We can then take Jesus' framework and apply it in our parenting.

Allow me to tell you two stories. The first is mine. The second is Peter's.

———————

It was the most humiliating morning of my life, bar none. And the craziest part was that no one was even there to witness it except Jesus and me.

I was the pastor of a church named Messiah in a little community south of Midland, Michigan, called Bullock Creek. Remarkably, from 1990 to 2000 the congregation grew by over 1000 in weekly worship. It was an insanely busy time. And I was just a baby pastor. I was 26 years old, and Messiah was my first congregation. I had been assigned there out of the seminary in 1989. I really didn't know what I was doing, except I was enthusiastic, and I wanted to help people meet Jesus.

At the first worship service I led, Susan counted 52 people. But God started bringing more. By the end of the second year, we needed to add a second service. But God kept bringing more. After another year, the congregation started building an addition to make more room. And God kept bringing more.

At the same time, I was scrambling to try and keep up with leading and discipling all the new people. I soon enrolled in a training program out of Wilmore, Kentucky which introduced me to pastors and leaders who had experience in leading growing congregations. They taught me both how to facilitate the congregation's continued growth and how to keep growing my personal relationship with Jesus.

It was during this season that Jesus began messing with me about spending more time with him in prayer. I knew I should do it. It made a lot of sense. People I admired said they couldn't survive the busy life of a growing congregation without it. In fact, at various training conferences, I wrote in my notes: "Start a regular prayer time." I even began underlining it in my notes for emphasis (as if that would help). However, I fell into a common pattern. At the conferences, I would get all fired up to start a prayer time; but when I got home, I found myself too busy to actually start.

Or so I thought.

You see, the real reason I was "too busy" for a prayer time was not my full schedule; it was that I was full of myself. I was polite about it. Pastoral even. To the congregation, I simply looked hard working and energetic. But I was definitely full of myself. And my lack of commitment to prayer was a symptom of it. It wasn't that I didn't have time to pray; it was that I was quietly convinced that I could handle the challenges of the church on my own. I had energy. I had answers. I had vision. In my mind, Jesus was invaluable, but I was indispensable. And day after day, I ignored prayer while using up all my energy being indispensable.

However, Jesus was serious about having more facetime with me. So, he set me up. The congregation had once again outgrown their worship space and realized that adding another service was less expensive than adding another building project. So, the leaders decided to add a third service to our Sunday morning schedule. *However,* I thought that if three services were good, adding a *fourth* service had to be even better. I didn't pray about it. I didn't ask Jesus about it. I just pushed for it, *presuming* our growth would be accelerated. It was a no-brainer, right?

Well, plans were made, the new schedule was announced, and the appointed Sunday arrived. The first three services were packed, so I had high hopes for service #4. But only 20 people showed up for it. I was disappointed but thought maybe word would spread about how awesome the service had been and the next Sunday would be much better. It was not. In fact, only 12 people came the next Sunday.

Oh, oh. What was happening? I thought the plan was solid and should have worked. But when the third Sunday rolled around, do you know how many people showed up? Zero. I mean, not even Jesus showed up.

As I sat utterly alone in the sanctuary, I was crushed. I was humiliated. I was embarrassed. And I knew what Jesus was doing. He had been pressing me to have more intentional time with him in prayer, but I was too busy, too sure, too full of myself. I needed to be humbled. And he obliged – graciously even – by allowing the fourth service to fail so completely that no one was even there to notice.

Except for him and me.

Now, it's important to understand that while the experience was indeed humiliating and painful for me, Jesus' goal was not my humiliation or pain. His goal was to humble me so I would be blessed with more room for him and his Kingdom in my life. However, to get there, it was necessary for me to first experience the pain of coming to the end of my rope. I had to experience Proverbs 11:2 in real time, "When pride comes, then comes disgrace, but with humility comes wisdom."

And what wisdom came with the humility? I realized I had failed because I had failed to humbly pray to the Lord and to seek counsel from others. That doesn't mean the fourth service would have been packed if I had just prayed and sought counsel. It means I would have had the room in my head and heart to listen for direction from Jesus and others rather than operating like I was the smartest person in the room.

As I sat alone in the sanctuary, my ego was finally deflated enough to make prayer my priority. But I knew I couldn't do it on my own. I needed help. I needed a prayer partner who would pray with me and hold me accountable to this new way of life. I even realized that I couldn't trust myself to identify such a person on my own. I needed Jesus to do it for me.

So, I prayed. And, I did something new. I humbly waited on Jesus.

About 10 days later, in the middle of the afternoon, I was sitting in my church office, and I heard a tentative knock on my door. It was a man named Jay. He and his family were members of the congregation, but I didn't know him all that well. He came in looking nervous and unsure. I asked what had brought him by my office in the middle of the afternoon? He began to share with me an idea. He knew it sounded a little out-of-the-box, and he apologized for it. But he was wondering if I had ever thought of having a prayer partner.

I started to laugh.

Immediately, he apologized again and started backing out of my office. I said, "No, Jay, wait! You don't understand. I'm not laughing at your idea. I am laughing at what Jesus is up to here. Let me tell you a story..."

Starting that very day, Jay and I became prayer partners, and for the next 10 years he helped me be accountable and humble. Not only that, but Jesus also used our partnership to help build prayer into the culture of the congregation. We helped hundreds of other people connect with each other as prayer partners. We started inviting prayer partners to come to the church on Sunday mornings to pray for all the services and all the people. We had prayer partners stationed at the altar during every service who would come alongside anyone who wanted prayer. Soon, parents were kneeling at the altar with their kids and praying over them themselves. It was beautiful and powerful.

And it would have never happened if Jesus hadn't lovingly, precisely humbled me. "You're blessed when you're at the end of your rope. With less of you there is more of God and his Kingdom." As I reflect on that morning in the sanctuary, and how Jesus set me up to teach me the value of humility, I see his general framework in play: he was clear about *what* he was doing and *why* he was doing it.

I wish I could tell you this painful experience finally turned me into a reliably humble person. It did not. I certainly learned the value and wisdom of humility that morning, but there are many more stories of Jesus having to deflate my ego over the years to get it out of the way. (Sadly, egos in general grow back and grow back quickly.) The key is that while each lesson in humility was painful, Jesus loved me enough to keep at it. As a result, I have come to trust the wisdom of humbling myself. I don't always remember to do that, and my ego can quickly re-inflate and get in the way...again. But the faster I can remember to humble myself...again... and set my ego aside, the sooner I get to participate in the greater good which the Father has prepared.

In training me to be humble, Jesus was clear about *what* he was doing, *why* he was doing it, and loved me enough to *keep at it*. Peter learned that same lesson during his time with Jesus and learned it the same way: the hard way. That's probably why I resonate with Peter's story. I recognize my own in his. Perhaps you will too.

Peter's Story

Let's start with where Peter ended up. He states it himself in 1 Peter 5:5-6, "'God opposes the proud but gives grace to the humble.' Humble yourselves, therefore, under God's mighty hand, that he may lift you up in due time. Cast all your anxiety on him because he cares for you." He is convinced of this wisdom. He understands it. He trusts it. He practices it.

But not at first.

When Peter's training begins, he has an ego that is proud, robust, and usually gets in the way. Jesus certainly has his work cut out for him. However, the good news is that Jesus knew *what* he was doing, *why* he was doing it, and loved Peter enough to *keep at it*.

During his early days with Jesus, Peter heard a great deal about "the first being last and the last first" and "the greatest being least and the least greatest" and "those who exalt themselves being humbled and those who humble themselves being exalted." And I'm sure Peter nodded in agreement every time. I'm sure he thought, "That makes sense." But while hearing about humility is important, it is not the way Peter (or our families) will actually *become* humble.

Jesus knows who Peter will be once he finally comes to the end of himself, once he learns to trust the wisdom of setting his ego aside and putting his full confidence in the *Right Person* (God). Jesus can see the "Acts 2 version" of Peter. He can see the "1 Peter 5 version" of Peter. But to get there, Peter will first need to feel the pain of his ego being deflated.

And, so, Jesus obliges.

We have already witnessed a couple of examples. Peter's ego was deflated when he was frightened in the storm and had to hear Jesus ask him, "You of little faith, why are you so afraid?" (Remember Matthew 8?) Then, Peter's ego was deflated again when he sank into the water after the exhilaration of walking on it and had to hear Jesus ask him, "You of little faith, why did you doubt?" (Remember Matthew 14?)

In each case, Jesus was clear about *what* he was doing, *why* he was doing it, and loved Peter enough to *keep at it*. While the experiences were, indeed, humiliating, and painful for Peter, Jesus' goal wasn't to crush him but to coach him. Peter needed to feel the pain of his ego being crushed *so that* he would be ready to be coached in how to experience more of God and his Kingdom in his life.

And that brings us to the conversation recorded in Matthew 16:13-28. Jesus has just asked his trainees, "Who do people say that I am?" After they share what they've been hearing, Jesus then puts the same question to them, "But what about you? Who do you say I am?" And it is Peter who answers first and forcefully, "You are the Christ, the Son of the living God."

Jesus is pleased and says, "Blessed are you, Simon son of Jonah, for this was not revealed to you by man, but by my Father in heaven." And Jesus goes on to say some pretty fantastic things about his plans for Peter and this heaven-inspired confession. However, Peter will need more training in humility before those plans can come to pass.

How do we know? Because of what happens next.

Immediately after praising Peter, Jesus goes on to explain to his trainees what being "the Christ, the Son of the living God" will mean. It will mean that "he must go to Jerusalem and suffer many things at the hands of the elders, chief priests and teachers of the law, and that he must be killed and on the third day be raised to life." This is what the Father has prepared in advance for him to do. It will require humbling himself under the Father's mighty hand and putting great trust in him, but Jesus is willing and ready to do it.

And that's when it happens. Having heard what sounds to Peter like a very pessimistic plan, he takes Jesus aside and begins to "rebuke" him. Yes, you read that right. Peter is still so sure of himself and full of himself, he takes it upon himself to scold Jesus, the Son of the living God, and tell him how things need to be: "Never, Lord! This shall never happen to you!"

So, Jesus has to humble Peter...again. He turns on him and says, "Get behind me, Satan! You are a stumbling block to me; you do not have in mind the things of God, but the things of men."

Wow. Humiliating. Crushing. Painful. But absolutely necessary. Peter's ego is a stumbling block to Jesus' purpose. Again, Jesus knows what he is doing and why he is doing it. He loves Peter and his goal is not to crush him but to coach him. Jesus has big plans for his trainee, but they can't come to pass as long as Peter continues to let his ego take over. He needs to learn how to humble himself under God's mighty hand, so that *God* can lift him up and work through him in due time.

So, Jesus immediately uses the pain from Peter's crushing to once again coach him, "If anyone would come after me, he must deny himself and take up his cross and follow me. For whoever wants to save his life will lose it, but whoever loses his life for me will find it," (Matthew 16:24-25).

In other words, "Peter, if you want to find the fruitful and fulfilling life I told you about a few minutes ago, you have to first deny that big, proud, selfish ego of yours. It only gets in the way of you responding to what the Father is preparing for you to do. The reason I am going to Jerusalem to suffer, die, and rise, is because it is what the Father has prepared for me to do. To take up my cross, I must first take up humility. If you want to follow me, you must follow my example of humility. If you think you can both follow me and save your big ego, you are wrong. You have to choose."

I wish I could tell you this painful experience finally turns Peter into a reliably humble person. It does not. Not by itself. Not yet. By Matthew 18, he and the other trainees are again arguing about who is greatest (and Jesus coaches them to become humble like a little child). By Matthew 20, they are still jockeying for who will have the best position beside Jesus in his Kingdom (and Jesus coaches them to become great by becoming servants). By the time we see them in the upper room the night before Jesus' crucifixion (John 13), everyone is expecting someone else to start washing feet (and Jesus keeps coaching them by getting up and washing their feet instead).

It might seem like these guys will never learn! But what we are seeing is the importance of Jesus keeping at it. No single lesson will permanently humble them. (Remember, egos grow back.) Learning to humble themselves doesn't happen in a day. It is something that adds up day after day. They followed Jesus for three years. They heard his teaching, they saw his example, they had to take their humiliating lumps, and Jesus loved them enough to keep coaching them.

It added up.

And by the time we see Peter and the other trainees in the Book of Acts, they are putting their training into practice. We see them setting aside their egos – their pride, their fear, their selfishness, their insecurity – so that they are willing and ready to respond to what the Father has prepared for them. They are following the example of Jesus.

Now that you know Peter's story, what he writes in 1 Peter 5 takes on new depth, "'God opposes the proud but gives grace to the humble.' Humble yourselves, therefore, under God's mighty hand, that he may lift you up in due time. Cast all your anxiety on him because he cares for you."

Peter is finally, truly convinced of this wisdom. He understands it. He trusts it. And he practices it. But it was because Jesus was clear about *what* he was doing, *why* he was doing it, and loved Peter enough to *keep at it*.

How to Apply Jesus' Framework with Our Children

Of course, we parents are wise to apply Jesus' framework as we raise our little trainees too. But how?

Earlier, we summarized Jesus' framework with the following:
He practices humility *himself*: humility is not just a lesson, it's a lifestyle. He understands that "What they see is what they'll be."

He is clear about *what* he is doing as he trains his followers: training someone in humility involves a measure of pain. And because being trained in humility is painful, it requires him to be careful.

He is clear about *why* he is doing it: the pain of learning humility has a payoff. Less of their selfishness, arrogance, and indifference means more room to receive God's abundance and more readiness to offer that abundance to others around them.

He loves his trainees enough to *keep at it*: training humility doesn't happen in a day, but day after day. So, he keeps watching for opportunities to coach them.

So, how do we go about it with our children?

Have the personal discipline to practice humility yourself.

"What they see is what they'll be."

If you want to see your children practice humility, they will need to see you practicing humility. So, let them see you practicing it daily.

Let them see you practice humility before God.

"Humble yourselves under God's mighty hand, that he may lift you up in due time." Let them see you go to him in prayer, seek his counsel in the Bible, acknowledge him for every blessing, and admit your wrongs before him. "He guides the humble in what is right and teaches them his way," Psalm 25:9. Your children need to see you do that so they can imitate you.

Let them see you practice humility with your spouse.

Let them see you serve each other, encourage each other, compromise with each other, and apologize to each other. Let them see you work through your differences with humility and love. "Everyone should be quick to listen, slow to speak and slow to anger, for man's anger does not bring about the righteous life that God desires," James 1:19. Your children need to see you do that so they can imitate you.

Let them see you practice humility when you are anxious.

Peter learned it the hard way: "Cast all your anxiety on him because he cares for you." In other words, if your anxiety comes from putting your trust in the wrong person (yourself), then humble yourself and put your trust in the Right Person (the

God who cares for you). Your children need to see you do that so they can imitate you.

Let them see you practice humility when you have said or done the wrong thing.
There are three short sentences that will serve you well: "I was wrong. Please forgive me. How can I make it right?" Your children need to see that from you so they can imitate you.

Finally, let them see you practice humility by joining Jesus on his mission.
Let them see you head into your busy day willing and ready to quickly humble yourself whenever you see an opportunity to love a person with the abundant love the Father has already given you. Let them see you quickly set aside your ego and your schedule so you can respond to the Father's timing. Your children need to see you do that so they can imitate you.

Be clear about *what* you are doing: understand that teaching humility involves a measure of pain for your children.

Don't underestimate how sharp a tool "pain" can be.
Yes, the pain is unavoidable because having an ego deflated is always going to be painful. And, yes, the pain is necessary because it is necessary to deflate the ego to make more room for God and other people in your children's lives. However, because it is painful, be careful.

Because it is painful, be careful your words do not come from your anger or frustration.

Don't underestimate the pain you are inflicting and respect your children enough to carefully think about *what* you will say and *how* you will say it. It is too easy to cut too deeply when you speak out of anger or frustration. And such wounds can last a lifetime. Your children cannot "unhear" what you say. Instead of being emotional, be intentional.

Because it is painful, be careful your words are not flippant or sarcastic.
Again, don't underestimate the pain you are inflicting, and respect your children enough to carefully think about *what* you will say and *how* you will say it. It is too easy to cut too deeply when your words are flippant or sarcastic. And such wounds can last a lifetime. Your children cannot "unhear" what you say. Instead of using sarcasm, use wisdom.

Because it is painful, choose your criticisms with great care.
Someone once said, "When you keep criticizing your kids, they don't stop loving you. They stop loving themselves." Yes, your children need to be corrected, but they also need to be built up. A child can easily be overwhelmed by a parent's numerous criticisms. Proverbs 12:18 reminds us, "The words of the reckless pierce like swords, but the tongue of the wise brings healing," So, be choosy with your corrections and generous with your affirmations.

Because it is painful, be clear that even your most carefully chosen words leave little wounds behind. So, be sure to circle back and attend to the healing of those wounds.

When I was a young boy, I spent too much time in the South Texas sun. As a result, I now must regularly have suspicious growths removed from my skin. These "removals" are necessary but they're still painful and leave little wounds behind. And if I don't attend to the healing of those little wounds, they can become infected or worse. So, after the removals, I am given instructions about "wound care" I am supposed to follow. Similarly, no matter how necessary it is to remove a "growth" of arrogance or selfishness from your child, understand that even your most carefully chosen words will leave little wounds behind. And if you don't attend to those wounds, they can become infected and grow into resentment, discouragement, or worse. So, don't underestimate or ignore your child's wounds. Circle back and follow the instructions for "wound care."

And what are the instructions for "wound care?"
Reinforce your child's True Identity in Christ.
Remind them that they are beloved and forgiven children of the heavenly King no matter what. Remind them of what Peter learned the hard way: that they can cast all their anxiety on God because he cares for them. And, of course, remind them of your unconditional love and forgiveness.

If they feel your words have cut too deeply, apologize and ask for their forgiveness.
By asking for forgiveness, you are respecting your child while still clearing the way to talk less emotionally about what has happened and why.

Reinforce the wisdom of being confidently humble.
Talk about why their ego needed to be deflated. Talk about what they were missing because they were focused on themselves. Talk about how God opposes the proud person but lifts up the humble person to do important things for others.

Remind them of examples they have seen from your life that show the foolishness of being arrogant, selfish, or indifferent and the wisdom of being humble.
This is another important reason you need to be practicing humility yourself.

Ask them what they have learned and what they will do next.
Help them talk about what they have learned from this painful experience. Help them clarify what wisdom they will be taking into the next opportunity God gives them...because God loves them enough to give them new opportunities.

Be clear about *why* you are teaching the painful lessons of humility: the pain has a payoff.

> **The pain of their egos being deflated has the payoff of them being ready to be coached in living confidently under God's mighty hand.**
> In chapter 12 we defined "humility" as the habit of looking at God and ourselves and then having the good sense to set ourselves aside and trust him more than we trust ourselves. When your children experience the pain of coming to the end of themselves, they will sometimes feel deflated, crushed, and even humiliated like Peter

did. But they will also be ready – ready to be coached by you in the wisdom of humbling themselves and trusting God's greater abilities.

The pain of becoming less selfish, arrogant, and indifferent has the payoff of creating more room to receive God's abundance and more readiness to offer that abundance to others.
Every morning, Jesus invites you and your children to join him on his mission. That means, in the midst of everything going on around you, you are the ones who are looking for people who need a little of what you have already received in abundance from the Father – his love, joy, peace, patience, kindness, grace, and truth. Ephesians 2:10 says that the Father prepares such people and opportunities in advance for you. As you and your children learn to humble yourselves, you will experience a remarkable increase in your willingness and readiness to generously offer the Father's abundance to others. And the *faster* you humble yourselves in a moment of opportunity, the more immediately you will be able to respond to the people the Father has prepared.

Finally, love your children enough to *keep at it*.

Keep watching for coaching opportunities in their everyday lives.
Training your children to become humble doesn't happen in a day, but rather day after day. It's not a lesson, it's a lifestyle. Peter didn't write, "Humble yourselves, therefore, under God's mighty hand, that he may lift you up in due time," after his first day of following Jesus. It took years of Jesus loving Peter and coaching Peter to get there. Likewise, training your children in humility

will require your attention, intentionality, and consistency day after day. And your love will keep you motivated to keep at it.

Remember, training our children to be humble is more an art than a science. That's why Jesus gives us a framework. It's a framework to guide us as we practice the art of deflating and building up, correcting and affirming, applying the law and applying the gospel. It's a tricky balance to get right, and we parents will mess up. But if we keep Jesus' framework before us, learn from our mistakes, and have the discipline to be motivated by our love (not our anger, frustration or impatience), we will have the great joy of seeing our children humbly responding to the opportunities the Father has prepared for them.

HERE'S THE POINT

It's important for us parents to train our children to humble themselves faster as they join Jesus on his mission. Unfortunately, there's only one way to be trained in humility: the hard way. Because the process for learning humility is always painful, it is a tricky balance for us to get right with our children. The good news is that in the gospels Jesus shows us a simple framework for training humility:

Jesus practices humility *himself.*

He is clear about *what* he is doing as he trains his followers.

He is clear about *why* he is doing it.

He loves his trainees enough to *keep at it.*

SUSAN'S SNIPPETS

As parents, we often would like to protect our kids from any pain or hurt feelings. But God says, "When you pass through the waters, I will be with you; and when you pass through the rivers, they will not sweep over you," Isaiah 43:2. Our kids are watching as we go through humbling experiences and God lifts us up and blesses us through each of them. This helps them recognize God is with them and lifting them up in their own hard stuff as well.

C.S. Lewis once wrote, "The great thing, if one can, is to stop regarding all the unpleasant things as interruptions of one's 'own' or 'real' life. The truth is of course that what one calls the interruptions are precisely one's real life...the life God is sending day by day." (*The Letters of C. S. Lewis to Arthur Greeves*)

CHAPTER 14

GROWING ABILITY: DISCIPLING YOUR CHILDREN TO USE THEIR SUPERPOWER

"The student is not above the teacher, but everyone who is fully trained will be like his teacher."

—Jesus in Luke 6:40

You and your children have a superpower from God.

No, you are not superhuman, nor are you superheroes. But you do have a superpower: love. Why is love a superpower?

According to 1 John 4:7-8, love comes *from* God and God *is* love. Because love comes *from* God and *is* God, that makes love a bona fide superpower. Think about it: God's love literally transforms human beings from the inside out. Anger doesn't do it. Disapproval doesn't do it. Shame doesn't do it. The only thing that changes a human being from the inside out is God's love. Love changed you, and it will be love that ultimately changes any other human being.

And that's why Jesus wants us to train our children to use it as they join him on his mission. God's love is their superpower. It works. But it only works if they use it. So, how do we train our children to use it? By following Jesus' third discipling priority: "Growing Ability." (Check out the illustration from chapter 5.)

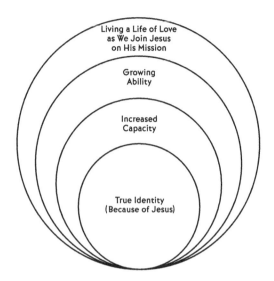

Each of Jesus' discipling priorities builds on the others to train our children to use their superpower as they join him on his mission:

True Identity – first, we work to convince our children of their true identity, value, and purpose, which are redeemed and restored through Jesus' death and resurrection. The more convinced they become of their true identity in Christ, the more they are set free to live in the abundance of God's love without reservation or uncertainty as they join Jesus on his mission.

TRUE IDENTITY = CONVINCED THEY HAVE
RECEIVED GOD'S ABUNDANT LOVE, WHICH IS THEIR
SUPERPOWER

Increased Capacity – second, we work to increase our children's capacity for trusting God more and humbling themselves faster. By knowing how to counter their fear and pride with trust and humility, our children are more willing and ready to use their superpower generously on others as they join Jesus on his mission.

INCREASED CAPACITY = WILLING AND READY TO USE THEIR SUPERPOWER GENEROUSLY ON OTHERS

Growing Ability – finally, we work to grow our children's ability to use their superpower on others by helping them practice the following skills:

1. Seeking the Kingdom
2. Hearing from Jesus in the Gospels
3. Talking with People
4. Doing Good
5. Ministering through Prayer

We call these skills the "Five Mission Practices." They put our children into better position to seek, recognize, and respond in love to what the Father is already doing in the lives of people around them. The more they improve practicing these skills, the more confident and effective they will become as they join Jesus on his mission and use their superpower on others.

GROWING ABILITY = IMPROVING THEIR SKILLS FOR USING THEIR SUPERPOWER ON OTHERS

Why focus on these "Five Mission Practices" or skills? Let's take a look.

Five Mission Practices

1. Seeking the Kingdom
    "Seek first the kingdom of God," Matthew 6:33.
    "I tell you, open your eyes and look," John 4:35.

"Seeking the Kingdom" is the first skill we want our children to develop. Why? Because God is already on the move in the lives of people around them. He is already preparing people for our children to notice and love. "Seeking the Kingdom" is simply looking for and recognizing these opportunities.

It's important for parents to keep this skill very simple and concrete for our children. After all, according to Jesus, "Seeking the Kingdom" isn't a complicated, abstract concept. It's a simple, concrete activity which even a little child can do (Matthew 18:3-4). Jesus says they simply need to open their eyes and look (John 4:35). He says if they seek it, they will find it (Matthew 7:7). Anyone with faith can do it. If our children believe Jesus is alive and on the loose in the lives of people around them, they can seek the Kingdom too!

That's why we want to keep it concrete. Seeking the Kingdom isn't about looking for invisible things our children *cannot* see. It's about looking for the concrete things they *can* see with their eyes and hear with their ears. Our children can't see what's going on inside of playmates, classmates, or teammates, but they can see expressions on faces. They can see circumstances. They can see behaviors. They can ask questions and listen carefully to answers. They can learn the stories of their friends and neighbors.

Then, at dinnertime or bedtime, you can ask your children about what happened during their day. Real experiences. Real people. Real opportunities. Real conversations. Real laughter. Real hardship. And with those concrete experiences in mind, you can talk with them about what Jesus was up to in the middle of it all. What opportunities was he giving? What were they able to say or do in response?

As your children grow in their skill to look for and recognize what God is up to in the lives of people around them, they will become more intentional and effective at using their superpower on others. Your children can't fix their friends or solve all their problems, but when they offer a listening ear, a kind word, a helping hand, or a little news that's good, God goes to work doing what only God can do.

And it all starts with simply paying attention to what's already going on around them.

2.   Hearing from Jesus in the Gospels

"The words I have spoken to you are spirit and they are life,"
John 6:63.
"Why do you call me, 'Lord, Lord,' and do not do what I say?"
Luke 6:46
"The only thing that counts is faith expressing itself through love,"
Galatians 5:6.

The second skill we want to help our children develop is "Hearing from Jesus in the Gospels." If we want our children to be able to recognize what Jesus is showing them as they join him on his mission, then it starts with getting to know Jesus in the gospels. What Jesus said in the gospels he is still saying today. And what Jesus did in the gospels he is still doing today. So, the more our children get to know Jesus in the gospels, the better they will become at recognizing the opportunities he presents them to use their superpower.

Again, it is important for us to keep this skill very simple and concrete for our children. Someone once said that the Bible is shallow enough for a child to wade in but deep enough to drown a theologian. That's about right! So, keep it simple. When you are reading the gospels (or a Bible story book) with your children, focus on helping them to answer these two questions:

What is Jesus giving me to believe?

What is Jesus giving me to do for others?

When we read the gospels, Jesus is speaking to us. We are not studying Jesus; we are listening to Jesus. So, what is Jesus telling us we can believe and do?

For instance, let's say you and your children are reading about Jesus healing the paralytic in Mark 2 (either in the Bible or in a Bible story book). Four men carried their paralyzed friend to a house where Jesus was teaching. But there were so many people crowding around, they couldn't get their friend anywhere near Jesus. So, they went up on the roof, opened a hole, and lowered him down. Then Jesus surprised everyone by saying, "Son, your sins are forgiven." You can read the rest in Mark 2:1-12.

After reading the account with your children, you could ask them, "What is Jesus giving us to believe?" They might say something like, "Jesus has the power to forgive our sins." Then you could ask, "What is Jesus giving us to do for others?" They might say, "Help our friends meet Jesus so they can believe their sins are forgiven too!" Then you could say, "Let's ask Jesus to help us do that for our friends today."

With these clear instructions from Jesus, your children can head into their day knowing what Jesus is giving them to believe and looking for what he is giving them to do for others. The more they improve at this skill, the more effective and confident they will become at joining Jesus on his mission and using their superpower of God's love.

One quick tip: when you are reading the Bible, don't worry about what you or your children do not understand. Focus on what you *do* understand. Martin Luther once advised his congregation that if they were reading Scripture and came across something they did not understand, they should commend it to God, thank him for it, and keep reading. (See *"Sermons on the Gospel of St. John"*). In other words, don't let the unclear parts of the Bible distract you from what the clear parts are giving you to believe and do.

After all, Jesus says the whole Bible can be summed up in this, "Love the Lord with all your heart and your neighbor as yourself," (Matthew 22:37-40). And Paul says it this way, "The only thing that counts is faith expressing itself through love," (Galatians 5:6).

That we can all understand and put into practice for the good of others.

3.   Talking with People
"When a Samaritan woman came to draw water, Jesus said to her..."
John 4:7.

"It's hard not to like someone once you know their story."
—Mr. Rogers

The third skill we want to help our children develop is "Talking with People." This skill focuses on learning the stories of their friends. It's natural for our children to overlook the deeper thoughts, experiences, and beliefs their friends may have. However, the more they learn about their friends' stories, the better insights they will have for how to use their superpower of love on them.

For example, when our family moved to Houston in 2007, our daughter, Ellen, was about to begin the third grade. We registered her in our local public school and on the first day of classes walked into a room full of smiling third graders.

And Ellen knew none of them.

So, we supported her as she started the slow but steady work of getting to know the new kids in her life. Who are these new classmates? What are their names? What are their stories? What are their families like? What do they believe?

Throughout elementary, middle, and high school, Ellen learned their stories. She learned about their experiences, feelings, and beliefs – including that many were not followers of Jesus. Some were Muslim, some were Hindu, and some were atheists. As Ellen learned their stories, she found herself in better position to use her superpower of love. She couldn't fix them, save them, or solve all their problems, but she could love them. Ellen's friends felt seen by her, heard by her, and valued by her.

Since high school graduation, some of Ellen's classmates have reached out to her. They wanted her to know that they had become followers of Jesus and were baptized. They wanted her to know how God used the conversations from years before to continue working in their heads and hearts.

"Talking with People" is a simple skill to learn. But by practicing it, our children will find themselves in a better position to use their superpower and become participants in the bigger story of what God is up to in the lives of their friends.

4.   Doing Good
     "For we are God's workmanship, created in Christ Jesus to do good works, which God prepared in advance for us to do." Ephesians 2:10.

     "You are the light of the world. A city on a hill cannot be hidden.
     Neither do people light a lamp and put it under a bowl. Instead, they put it on its stand, and it gives light to everyone in the house. In the same way, let your light shine before [people], that they may see your good deeds and praise your Father in heaven," Matthew 5:14-16.

The Bible teaches us three things about "Doing Good." Jesus talks about all three in Matthew 5:14-16.

1. Doing good is a result of who you are.
2. Doing good is how people are able to "see" and experience God's love.
3. Doing a little good can make a big difference to others.

First, doing good is a result of who you are. Jesus says, "You are the light." He doesn't say, "Try to be the light," or "Learn to be the light." He says, "You already are the light" because of something you already have, namely, the abundant love of God. Remember your true identity in Christ: you are a beloved child of the heavenly King. To other people, the abundant love you already have is a bright light. Like a city on a hill. Like a lamp that lights up a home. So, Jesus says, because that's who you are, do what you do. "Let your light shine before people."

And how do we do that? Jesus covers that next.

He says, "Let your light shine before people, that they may *see your good deeds*..." How will people be able to "see" your light, which is his love? Jesus says by what you do. "Doing Good" puts his love into action so others will literally be able to "see" and experience God's love through you.

Finally, because you are "the light," you and your children don't have to attempt big, impressive acts of goodness for your light to be seen. After all, a *little* light makes a big difference. And if it only takes a little, then little children can use their superpower and let their light shine too. In fact, that's exactly what Jesus teaches: do small things with God's great love. He says those small acts of love are like seeds that are sown (Matthew 13:3), a pinch of yeast that is mixed in (Luke 13:21), a cool cup of water that is offered (Matthew 10:42), or a lamp put on its stand (Matthew 5:15).

Several years ago, I was asked to speak at a gathering of 1,200 children from various Christian elementary schools. Before the event began, I asked the lighting technician if he could do me a favor. I asked him if it would be possible to turn out all the lights in the theater when I gave him my cue? He said he could do that.

During my presentation, I taught the children about Jesus' words in Matthew 5. I taught them that because they have God's love, they already are his light. And even a little bit of his light can make a big difference to others. I then took a moment to light a solitary match and held it up. It was just one flame. In fact, the kids could barely see its light. That is, until I gave the technician my cue. Suddenly the whole theater was plunged into darkness. And, yet, despite the theater now being filled with several thousand cubic feet of darkness, everyone was able to see that one small flame shining brightly.

Mother Teresa put it this way, "Not all of us can do great things. But we can do small things with great love." She was right. And she got it from Jesus.

5.   Ministering through Prayer
   "Thy kingdom come, thy will be done on earth as it is in heaven."
   – Jesus in Matthew 6:10.

   "When we work, we work. When we pray, God works."
   – John Maxwell

When I was a young Daddy, I made a commitment that every morning the names of my wife and children would be heard in the throne room of my heavenly King. I liked to get up early and spend time in what I called my "prayer chair," praying for them, reading the Bible, and reflecting. I also prayed with my children every night before they went to bed (see "Circle Up" in chapter 15).

When Ellen, our youngest, started middle school, I added to those prayer habits. My "prayer chair" sat in a little study by the front door. Every morning, when she came running down the stairs to leave, I would call her in and pray with her. It took less than 60 seconds, but I wanted her to leave with a blessing and a reminder of her true identity in Jesus. (An early version of a cheer-creed.)

In high school, Ellen's mornings became even more rushed. One morning, she tried hurrying out the door without stopping for prayer. She protested that she didn't have time for it. "Daaaad, I have to go! The bus is coming!" I looked at her and noticed she had pants on. So, I asked, "Would you leave the house without first putting on your pants?" "What?!" she asked. I clarified, "Would you ever be so short on time that you would consider leaving the house without first putting on your pants?" "Of course, not!" she replied indignantly. "So, somehow there's always time to put on your pants, right?" I confirmed. "Yes! I wouldn't leave the house without my pants on, Daaaad." (Imagine an exasperated tone accompanied by a colossal eyeroll.)

It was time to make my point, "It's the same with prayer. Just like you always have time to put on your pants before leaving the house, we always have time to cover you in prayer. We don't leave the house without our pants on and we don't leave the house without prayer. Good?"

"Okaaaaay. But can you at least hurry?"

Every morning after that, if she tried to leave without praying together, all I had to say was, "Don't leave without your pants on!" And it worked. She remembers the saying to this day. And, most importantly, she has become a woman of prayer herself.

While praying with your family may be a no-brainer, what about the people he has placed around you who are living without his grace and truth: your neighbors, your children's playmates, classmates, and teammates? Who's praying for them?

It could be you and your children.

Prayer is a way for your family to use its superpower on your neighbors and friends. It's a simple but powerful way to help them. There's certainly some mystery surrounding the gift of prayer. But this much is crystal clear: Jesus invites you to do it in his name for the good of others (John 14:13). Indeed, the key to prayer is not understanding it but doing it. When your family prays for neighbors and friends, you are literally changing their status quo. How? By inviting God's Kingdom to come and his will to be done in their lives.

He's a game-changer.

There are two ways to practice the skill of "Ministering through Prayer." You and your children can pray *for* friends and *with* friends. In other words, you can pray *for* friends every day during your family prayer time, and you can pray *with* friends in person as God gives opportunity. By the way, prayer is number 5 on the list not because it is the least important mission skill, but because when you put the other four skills into play, you will then have a better idea of *how* you can pray for and with your friends.

Praying *for* Friends

Like any other skill, the best way to grow your family's ability to pray is by practicing together. So, consider your family prayer time the place everyone gets to practice. Keep it simple. Don't worry about what words to use. What's important is not getting your words right but inviting your King in.

Start your prayer time by praying for each other. Sit in a circle and have each family member take a turn asking the person on their right,

"How can I help you with prayer?" Afterwards, each person can then lift up their partner's request in the name of Jesus.

Next, pray for the neighbors, playmates, classmates, and teammates God has placed in your family's life – especially those living without the grace and truth of Jesus. In the Appendix at the back of the book, there is a Neighborhood Prayer Map which can help your family practice praying for neighbors and friends. As your family prays, write down the following on your map:

> The prayer needs of neighbors and friends and the dates you begin praying for them.

> As the list grows, don't feel pressure to pray every day for every person. Instead, pray for one person per day with the goal of working through your list once a week.

> Finally, watch for what God does. Be sure to write down whatever answers you and your children see. Note the date too. Those answered prayers will serve as powerful reminders and motivators for continued prayer.

Praying *with* Friends

Praying *with* friends in person is an effective way for your children to use their superpower (James 5:16). But first they have to get in position.

Here's how it works. As your children intentionally practice the first four mission skills, they will be growing friendships and deepening trust. In due time, as God gives opportunity, friends will start sharing what is really going on in their lives. Why? Because they know your children care. And, when friends share, one of the ways your children can offer to help is with prayer. After all, they've been practicing. They've already been praying *for* them during your family prayer time. It's time to pray *with* them.

When their friends share, your children can take the next step and say something like, "You probably don't know this, but I pray for you nearly every day. Would it be okay for me to pray with you right now?" And whether they pray together in the backyard, playground, or classroom, the Kingdom comes and the will of the Father is done right there as it is in heaven.

Helping your children develop the skill of prayer is a lifelong gift to them and to the people God brings across their path.

———————

So, those are the Five Mission Practices. They put your family into better position to seek, recognize, and respond in love to what the Father is already doing in the lives of people around you. The more you improve practicing these skills, the more confident and effective you will become as you join Jesus on his mission and use your superpower on others.

Now that we've unpacked Jesus' three discipling priorities – True Identity, Increased Capacity, and Growing Ability – it's time to introduce his Discipling Rhythm. It's a simple, sustainable way for you to weave his discipling priorities into your family's daily life.

And the best thing about it? It's simple and it works!

HERE'S THE POINT

God's love is our children's superpower. But it only works if they use it. So, how can we train our children to use their superpower on others? By following Jesus' third discipling priority: "Growing Ability." We work to grow our children's ability to use their superpower by helping them practice the following skills: Seeking the Kingdom, Hearing from Jesus in the Gospels, Talking with People, Doing Good and Ministering through Prayer (also known as the Five Mission Practices).

SUSAN'S SNIPPETS

You can use hand motions to help your family remember the Five Mission Practices. On our website, www.dwelling114.org, there is a video of Susan teaching these hand motions. Click the "Training Tools" dropdown menu, click "Joining Jesus as a Family," and scroll down to the video button.

Seeking the Kingdom: Looking
Place a hand above your eyes like you're looking for the King at work.

Hearing from Jesus in His Word: Listening
Cup hands around your ears like you're listening to Jesus, then bring them down to form an open book.

Talking with People: Talking
Cup hands around your mouth.

Doing Good: Helping
Open your hands and hold them out to serve others.

Ministering in Prayer: Praying
Hold your hands together in prayer.

CHAPTER 15

JESUS' DISCIPLING RHYTHM: TEACH, SHOW, SEND, AND CIRCLE UP

"We have come to understand we don't have to choose
*between family **or** mission.*
*We don't have to try to balance family **and** mission.*
*Instead, we are learning how to become a family **on** mission."*

—Bob Rognlien

I recently had a conversation with a mom who asked, "Do you want to hear how Jesus was messing with me the other day?" (I never get tired of hearing such stories.) Here's what she told me.

It was a Thursday afternoon around 5:00 p.m. She had been late picking up her kids from their middle school practices because it had been a crazy day at work. Before heading home, she needed to make a quick stop at the grocery store to grab something for dinner. As she was looking for a parking space, a car suddenly backed out and T-boned her car. Great. Just great. Everyone was okay, but what an inconvenience. So, she gets out of her car to see what the damage is and realizes the guy who hit her is someone she actually knows. They went to high school together.

The guy recognizes her too and begins apologizing profusely. In fact, he becomes distraught. He explains that he's been under a lot of stress lately. Things are rough. The mom recognizes that Jesus may be up to something here. So, she takes a deep breath, says a prayer, and listens.

As the guy is talking, lo and behold, who should walk out of the store but the mom's pastor! She waves him over and introduces him to her old classmate. The pastor talks with him for a few minutes and they agree to set up a time when they can meet and talk some more.

As the mom gets back in her car, the kids are high-fiving each other and yelling, "Can you believe what Jesus just did?! That's so COOL!"

The mom said to me, "Truth be told, it *was* pretty cool. Dinner was late, the car needed repairs, and the day in general was a disaster. But, yeah, it was pretty cool to join Jesus on his mission and have my kids see it unfold. The only question I have is," she asked with a wry smile, "why didn't Jesus have the man T-bone my pastor's car rather than mine?"

Joining Jesus on his mission is not one more thing a family does on *top* of everything else. It is what they do in the *midst* of everything else. It's not a church program. It's not a hobby. It's a daily lifestyle. And every day is a new adventure with Jesus. Sure, we go about our daily routines. We go to work. Our kids go to school. We go to the grocery store. But we go with Jesus. We go with a sense of awareness and anticipation because we just never know what Jesus may be up to!

Yes, the days are busy. But in the midst of all the running, we know who we are and what we are about. We are Jesus-followers. We are loved by the Father, and our mission is simple: we look for people who need a little of what we already have in abundance. "Freely you have received, freely give." And when we see such a person – a friend, a co-worker, an old classmate at the store – we get over ourselves and offer the person a cool cup of grace.

This is who our family is. This is what our family does. We are a family on mission with Jesus. And we're having a blast! At least that's the goal. But it is a challenge.

Families have a lot to juggle. Life comes at us fast. We want to disciple our children with Jesus' discipling priorities: True Identity, Increased Capacity, and Growing Ability. We want to disciple our children to join Jesus as part of their everyday lives. But is there a simple way to do that? Is there a simple way to intentionally weave his discipleship into our family's daily routine? A simple rhythm we can follow that keeps our family connected, encouraged, and on track with Jesus?

(Did I mention it needs to be something *simple*?) Thankfully, Jesus has something simple for us. And it works!

We see it in the gospels. Jesus has a simple discipling rhythm he uses with his trainees which he weaves into their daily routines. We can sum it up like this:

Teach them
Show them
Send them
Circle Up with them and share the stories

Pretty straightforward, right? Jesus **teaches** them what they need to know (Mark 1:15), **shows** them how to put it into practice by how he lives (Mark 1:18), **sends** them out to gain their own experience (Mark 3:14), and finally **circles up** with them to share the stories of what was discovered and learned (Mark 6:30). Simple but effective.

The result? Over time, day by day, Jesus' trainees gain experience and confidence in living a life of love and joining him on his mission...in other words, they get *better* at it. And you can imitate the same discipling rhythm with your family. You don't have to figure out a *new* way. You can just imitate *Jesus'* way.

Teach them what they need to know.

Show them how to put it into practice by how you live.

Send them into the day to gain their own experience.

Circle up and share the stories of what everyone discovered and learned as they joined Jesus.

JESUS' DISCIPLING RHYTHM = OUR FAMILY'S DISCIPLING RHYTHM

Here's how it works.

Teach Them

The discipling rhythm starts with telling our children what they need to know about faith. As Paul writes, "How can they believe unless they hear? Consequently, faith comes from hearing the message, and the message is heard through the word of Christ," (Romans 10:14-17).

But, of course, teaching the facts and figures of the faith to our own children is *precisely* what terrifies us the most! It sounds like a bad idea. All those characters, stories, details, and doctrines. "Shouldn't I leave it to the professionals? After all, I am *not* a biblical expert! What if I mess something up?"

However, here's the good news. Your children don't need you to be a biblical expert. What your children need from you *is to teach them why you trust and follow Jesus.* (You can partner with the biblical experts in your local congregation to teach the facts and figures of the faith to your children.)

Sure, there's plenty you don't know about the Bible. Even the so-called biblical experts don't know everything. But you *do* know Jesus. So, teach your children about why you trust and follow him. That's what Paul means when he says, "...the message is heard through the word of Christ." In other words, tell your children about Jesus.

My advice? Keep it simple. (And remember, you've got this because Jesus is with you.)

First, remember that your children experience and interpret their relationship with Jesus via their relationship with you. If they are going to believe Jesus loves, values, and enjoys them, at least part of the reason is because they have been experiencing those things through you. So, the "teaching" of your children starts with something as simple as telling them how much you love them. And doing it often. Telling them how proud you are of them. And telling them why. Telling them you enjoy hearing the stories of their day. And then listening attentively.

Second, "teaching" your children what they need to know is as simple as reminding them every day of their true identity, value, and purpose in Jesus. You can tell them, "Because Jesus died on the cross and rose again to take away your sins, this is who you are, this is what you have of value to offer others, and this is your true purpose. You are a beloved, forgiven child of the heavenly King. You have the superpower of his love. And you get to go on an adventure with Jesus today to see who you can help."

Third, don't worry about trying to be a biblical expert. Instead, be a fellow-learner with your children. You don't have to pretend to know more than you do. Be humble. Read Bible story books together, which simplify details in very helpful ways. Afterwards, to help the story sink in, you can have your children draw a picture of what they heard or use action figures to act it out. And when your children have a question, learn to reply with, "That's a good question. Let's find out together."

For parents with young children, the most natural time for reading Bible stories together is often at bedtime. The Finke children are grown up now, but they have fond memories of snuggling with Susan and me at bedtime and reading Bible stories together. This was how they first learned the characters, stories, and teachings of the Bible.

As children grow older, they will probably start to get a little bored with the same Bible stories. After all, you have read them together *hundreds* of times. So, that's when you can begin transitioning from simply reading the stories to having conversations *about* the stories. Don't leave the stories behind, instead read the stories and talk about the two questions introduced in chapter 14:

> What is Jesus giving us to believe?
>
> What is Jesus giving us to do for others?

One last tip. If you have these conversations with your children at the end of the day, it will be important to begin the next day with a brief reminder of what you talked about the evening before. The best time for unhurried conversations may be dinnertime or bedtime. But the next day is the best time for putting those insights into action.

So, teaching your children what they need to know is the first step of Jesus' discipling rhythm. It is the start. It is the catalyst. And now that they have heard, they can believe. But teaching them only gets the discipling rhythm rolling.

Now it's time to *show* them what you *told* them by putting it into practice in your daily life.

Show Them

Of course, you want your children to learn the facts and figures of the faith accurately – the characters, stories, details, and doctrines – but they also need you to show them what it looks like to live out the faith for the good of others as you join Jesus on his mission.

So, show them.

Show them how to live in the abundance of the Father's love, joy, and peace.

Show them how to be a Jesus-follower who enjoys life, laughs easily, and loves generously.

Show them how to join Jesus on his mission by noticing, valuing, and responding to the people around you.

Show them how to trust the Father more and humble yourself quickly.

Show them how to continue learning from Jesus by listening to him in the gospels and talking with him in prayer.

Show them how to practice hospitality with neighbors.

Show them, because they are watching.

During the riot that erupted in our community in May of 2020, there was much to lament. However, the next morning, I saw an interview with a Black father and his eight-year-old son. They were helping to clean up the community after the violence. The reporter asked the father why he had brought his son along with him. He replied, "I wanted my son to know what love looks like. He saw the violence. I wanted him to see the love. We came to see it and show it to our neighborhood."

Teach them the faith, yes, but show them the faith by how you live. And, then…it's their turn.

Send Them

When it comes to figuring out how to live their faith and join Jesus on his mission, your children need your words, and they need your example. But they also need an opportunity to give it a try on their own. It's the only way they can gain experience. So, the next step of the rhythm is to send your children into their day to join Jesus themselves.

Turns out, "sending" them to gain their own experience isn't that tricky. You're already doing it every day. The day care center is already a mission field. The carpool is already a mission field. The school is already a mission field. Soccer practice is already a mission field. And you're already sending them to those places.

So, send them with a sense of purpose: "Are you ready to have some fun joining Jesus on his mission? Good! Give me a high five. Now, remember who you are and the abundance you have from God. Be ready to trust him more and get over yourself quickly. Put your Five Mission Practices into play. And when you have the chance to help someone with your superpower, use it. You ready? Let the adventures with Jesus begin!"

And when the adventures of the day are complete? It's time for the final step of Jesus' daily discipling rhythm: circle up as a family and tell the stories.

Circle Up with Them

"So, what happened?" It's a simple question but an incredibly important one. It invites the stories. Children love to hear their parents' stories and they are eager to share their own.

After all, you and your children have had a full day of adventuring with Jesus. Everyone had places to be and things to do. But in the *midst* of it all, you were following Jesus and putting the Five Mission Practices into play: looking, listening, and responding to the people he brought across your path.

So, at the end of the day, Circle Up and ask, "What happened? What did you see? Who did you talk with? What was Jesus up to? What were you able to do?"

"Tell me the stories."

Parents have found that "Circle Up and Share the Stories" is actually the key to the whole discipling rhythm. Hearing and telling the stories helps children reframe all they have seen and heard during the day with Jesus in the middle of it. Here's how it works.

Circle up with them.

- Come together during a family meal, a walk, a drive to school, or before bed (see Deuteronomy 6:7).
- Put the phones aside and be present.
- Let the adrenaline drain off. Don't be in a hurry. R-e-l-a-x.
- If friends are with your children, invite them to join in.

Invite their stories by asking them questions.

- Ask, "So, what happened today? What did you see? Who did you talk with? What was Jesus up to? What did you do? What didn't go so well? What did you learn?"
- Inviting their stories affirms the importance of what happened during their day, especially the little things (see Matthew 13:3-9).
- One family we know follows a "Joy, Junk, Jesus" outline. Each person shares a story about what made them happy during the day (Joy), what made them sad or mad (Junk), and finally what they saw Jesus was up to and how they were able to join him. Usually, the "Joy" and "Junk" stories lead into the "Jesus" stories.
- If you have young children, they may need help remembering or understanding what happened during their day. So, take note of whenever you see them sharing, helping, showing kindness, etc. Then, during "Circle Up" time, you can say, "Here's what I saw you doing with Jesus today..." This helps make "joining Jesus"

more concrete for them and is positive reinforcement for their loving attitudes and behaviors.

- As children get older, many families choose to use the "Five Questions" which were introduced in our book, "Joining Jesus on His Mission." The questions prompt stories about what happened as they put the Five Mission Practices into play: seeking the Kingdom, listening to Jesus, talking with people, doing good, and ministering through prayer. You can find the questions at the end of the chapter. Also, on our website we provide age-appropriate language options for the Five Questions: www.dwellilng114.org under Tools/Joining Jesus as a Family.

- The stories of what your family missed or messed up are as important for learning as what went well. Remember, when you're a trainee of Jesus, failure isn't failure…it's training. So, admit mistakes, but be sure to help each other *learn* from them too.

Be ready to share your own stories.

- The lessons from your stories make more of an impression on your children than the lessons from your lectures. So, pay attention to what Jesus is up to during the day so you can share your stories during Circle Up.

- Telling your stories is another way to "show them" how you live your faith.

- Again, your "miss" stories are especially helpful for the discipling of your children. Your goal is not to show them how to be perfect but how to be a follower of Jesus. So, talk with them about your mistakes and about what you will do differently moving forward.

Read a Bible story together or continue reading in the gospels where you left off: Matthew, Mark, Luke, or John.

- Ask, "What is Jesus giving us to believe and what is he giving us to do for others?"
- Take notes. In the morning you will want to remind each other what Jesus told you.

Finish up with prayer.

- Go around and have each person ask, "How can I help you with prayer?"
- Then enjoy praying for each other.
- Also, pray for your neighbors, playmates, classmates, and teammates who are living without the grace and truth of Jesus.
- Use the Neighborhood Prayer Map (found in the Appendix) to write down the prayer needs of neighbors and friends and the dates you begin praying for them.
- As the list grows, don't feel pressure to pray every day for every person. Instead, pray for one person per day with the goal of working through your list once a week.
- Finally, watch for what God does. Be sure to write down whatever answers you and your children see. Note the date too. Those answered prayers will serve as powerful reminders and motivators for continued prayer.

Note: for those who have read our first two books, *Joining Jesus on His Mission* and *Joining Jesus: Show Me How*, think of "Circle Up" as your family's Missional Community time. "Circle Up" isn't a new thing we made up. It's a very old thing we simply rediscovered. In the gospels, we see Jesus incorporating it into his discipling rhythm. He intentionally gets his trainees out of the busyness of the day and the press of the crowds so they can have unhurried time for reflection and conversation with him.

We see Jesus "Circle Up" with his trainees when he gets them into a boat to "leave the crowds behind" and go "to a solitary place" (Mark 4:36; 6:32). We see Jesus "Circle Up" with his trainees when he leads them into a house where they can privately reflect on his teaching and ask their questions (Mark 7:17). We see it when Jesus uses the time it takes to travel by foot to talk with them about what is happening and what it means (Mark 8:27). We see it when they regularly gather at the Garden of Gethsemane to take a breather, talk, and pray (John 18:2; Luke 22:39).

So, with Jesus' example, it's not surprising that parents have found "Circle Up" to be the key to their family's discipling rhythm. Why does it work?

First, sharing the stories helps your children pull together all they are learning through Jesus' discipling rhythm. You have taught them, shown them, and sent them. So, what was Jesus up to? What did they experience? What did they learn? Without "Circle Up" time, the experiences and lessons of the day are often a blur and are quickly lost. However, sharing the stories helps your family process their day, better understand their experiences and lessons, and then anchors it all in their memory.

Second, because sharing the stories helps your children *process and remember* what Jesus was teaching them today, they will be better *prepared* for what happens tomorrow. Sharing their stories day by day helps them build experience and gain wisdom. Misses and mistakes still happen – a lot – but their capacities and abilities are growing too. Circling up and telling the stories reinforces that growth so your children are better prepared for tomorrow's adventures with Jesus.

Finally, sharing the stories helps your children learn how to recognize Jesus' presence and activity in their daily lives. By telling the stories, lightbulbs of insight pop on. They start realizing that opportunities they can see with their eyes have been prepared by the One they cannot see. The abstract becomes more concrete. The invisible more visible. The biblical more applicable. And Jesus is no longer just a story in their Bible, but he's someone they regularly "see" and experience in their daily lives.

Speaking of stories, let me tell you one.

It was August, 2010, and Ellen, our youngest, was preparing to enter middle school. She was nervous. It was a huge school, and she would be changing classes for the first time. She is a pretty strategic person, so when she went to orientation, she took note of where all her classrooms would be and determined which locker would be the best location for her. Later, during our Circle Up time, she told me how much she hoped she would get a certain locker: #263.

"Wow," I said, "You picked out the *specific* locker you want?" "Yeah," she replied, "#263. It would be so helpful. My classes are really spread out, and I'm worried I'll be late all the time. This locker is in the perfect place for me to switch my books and get to my next class on time. But I know I won't get it. All the seventh and eighth graders get their lockers first. Then the rest are randomly assigned to the sixth graders."

I saw an opportunity.

For some time, I had been trying to help Ellen connect the dots between her daily life and the presence and activity of Jesus. I had also been trying to help her embrace prayer as her first and best choice and not simply her last resort. We were making some progress, but middle school had her attention in a whole new way.

So, I said, "I know Someone who can get you locker #263." She was surprised, "You do?" But then she saw the look in my eyes and knew what I meant. "Daaaad." But I pressed on, "Hey, why not ask Jesus to guide this whole 'random' process?" And we did. Ellen and I put it in his hands, but we also boldly asked for locker #263.

She had her doubts.

A week later the assignments were posted. And do you know what? I kid you not, Ellen was assigned locker #263. Yep. Wow. Pretty cool, huh? Ellen had lived her whole life knowing she was a beloved daughter of the King. She knew her Bible stories well. She had our example. But this may have been the first time everything came together in such a concrete way. Dots were connected. It was specific. It was obvious. (Jesus likes to show off like that sometimes.)

It wasn't that the locker itself was such a big deal. It was that Jesus gave her such a personal example of his love and attention.

Now, fast forward six years to August of Ellen's senior year in high school. For years, we had woven Jesus' discipling rhythm into our family's daily routines: teach, show, send, circle up and share the stories. And because of that, Ellen had become experienced at recognizing Jesus in her daily life and joining him on his mission. She had confidence that the opportunities she could see with her eyes had been prepared by the One she could not see. By her senior year, the abstract had become more concrete. The invisible more visible. The biblical more applicable. And Jesus was no longer just a story in her Bible but someone she could regularly "see" and count on in her daily life.

Of course, discipling Ellen wasn't always smooth sailing, nor did she always appreciate it (in fact, looking back on it, she now laughs and says she was often quite annoyed by it), but the daily discipling rhythm kept us connected and growing as a family and as disciples of Jesus. She recently wrote, "I tell people a lot about how knowing you and mom would ask me every day about how God was working in my life made me actually look for him throughout the day."

And by her senior year, even though Jesus was not through with her yet, her growth was obvious.

So, back to the story: it's August of her senior year. She needs a parking permit because she's going to drive a car to school. She puts in the application. You'll never guess which parking spot was randomly assigned to her. That's right. #263

We all busted out laughing at how clever and cool this was! It's almost as if Jesus was winking at Ellen and saying, "Do you see what I did there? It was just for you." It was specific. It was obvious. (Jesus likes to show off like that sometimes.)

Like the locker in middle school, it wasn't that the parking spot itself was such a big deal. It was that Jesus wanted to give her such a personal reminder of how far she had come...with him...in relationship and mission. And for her mom and dad? It was pretty cool to be reminded of that too.

——————

Ellen has graduated from college now. About six months ago she left me a voicemail. It's easily my all-time favorite from her: "Hi Dad, I love you. I'm sorry I was such a butthead growing up. I was talking to people yesterday about how great I had it growing up. I said, yeah, my dad made me pray with him before I left the house for the day. He made me read the gospels with him. He would always ask me how I saw God at work in my life. And I was really annoyed about it at the time. But now it was literally the best thing you could have ever done for me. So, thanks. I'm sorry I was a butthead. But besides the Lord, you and Mom are the reason I am the way I am today. And it's not awful. So, thanks. I love you and I miss you. I'll talk to you soon. Bye."

HERE'S THE POINT

In the gospels, Jesus shows us a rhythm we can use to weave his discipling practices into our family's daily routine: teach them, show them, send them, and then circle up to share the stories. It's simple and it works.

SUSAN'S SNIPPETS

As our kids get older, I certainly enjoy hearing the occasional, "Sorry I was a butthead," or "Wow, you got that right!" As parents we may have to wait a long time for those kinds of comments, but they are sweet, sweet sounds in our ears when we do!

The 5 Questions

You can support each other as a family by using "The 5 Questions" to help prompt stories and conversations about how life on mission with Jesus is going. The questions are based on "The Five Mission Practices" which put us in position to join Jesus on His mission.

How did you see God at work in your life today?

What did he seem to be showing you? Who has he been bringing across your path? Who is he inviting you to notice and pay attention to?

What has God been teaching you in his Word?

As you read about Jesus in the gospels, what did he invite you to believe and do? What happened when you put it into practice for the good of others?

What kind of conversations are you having with your pre-Christian friends?

A conversation with anyone God brings across your path is important. But a conversation with someone living without the grace and truth of Jesus is especially important. What did you learn about the person's story?

What might be the next step with them?

What good can you do around here?

As you reflect on your observations and conversations with the people around you, how can you serve, bless, or encourage someone in the next few days?

How can we help you in prayer?

Prayer for and with each other is powerful and effective (James 5:16).

CHAPTER 16

JOINING JESUS ON HIS MISSION: WHO'S YOUR ONE?

"Suppose one of you has a hundred sheep and loses one of them."

—Jesus telling the story of the lost sheep in Luke 15:4

If your family wants to join Jesus on his mission, you don't have to wonder where to go.

You're already there.

Your mission field is your family's everyday life. It's your neighborhood, daycare, park, school, team, or workplace. It's the people already around you who are struggling to live without grace or truth. They just need you to notice their struggle and offer a little of what you already have in abundance.

Your job isn't to *save* them. (The Bible says you can't even save yourself. Why would you think it's up to you to save others?) Saving people is Jesus' job, not yours. But he does invite your family to join him on the adventure. How? By using your superpower, of course. The Bible calls it "loving your neighbor." But to take "joining Jesus" to the next level, your family will want to do one more thing Jesus does: prioritize lost sheep.

What?

In the gospels, while it's true Jesus loves everyone who comes across his path, he puts a *priority* on those who are lost, a.k.a., struggling without his Father's grace and truth. "For the Son of Man came to seek and to save what was lost," (Luke 19:10). He loves everyone, but his priority is seeking and saving the ones who are lost.

And it makes sense.

As parents, we would do the same thing. Susan and I have three children. If one of them got lost, we wouldn't go, "Oh well. We have two more." No, we would turn the world upside-down looking for our lost child! That doesn't mean we would suddenly love our other two children any less. It's just that the lost one must now become our top priority.

In Luke 15, Jesus appeals to this same logic. The religious types are giving him grief because he is "welcoming sinners and eating with them." But Jesus doesn't see lost sinners as people to avoid. Rather, he sees them as people to *prioritize*. So, Jesus tells a story, "Suppose one of you has a hundred sheep and loses one of them. Would he not leave the ninety-nine in the open country and go after the lost sheep until he finds it?"

Well, of course he would. It's not that the ninety-nine are suddenly less valuable to the shepherd. It's just that they are already *safe*. It's the lost one who must become the priority.

"And when he finds it, he joyfully puts it on his shoulders and goes home. Then he calls his friends and neighbors together and says, 'Rejoice with me; I have found my lost sheep!' I tell you that in the same way there will be more rejoicing in heaven over one sinner who repents than over ninety-nine righteous persons who do not need to repent."

The first part of Jesus' story is focused on the priority of "seeking and finding" lost sinners, and the rest of the story is focused on "rejoicing and celebrating" when we do.

Sounds like a pretty fun way to live, right?

So, like Jesus, we love whoever God brings cross our path. But if we want to take "joining Jesus" to the next level, if we want to see *heaven* get excited, if we want to have an *amazing* reason to celebrate with our Christian friends and neighbors, then we will make looking for lost sheep our family's priority too.

That's what Kaitlyn did.

I was recently working with a congregation in Missouri where I heard the story of two 15-year-olds. Let's call them "Kaitlyn and Allie" (not their real names). Kaitlyn made Jesus' priority her own and started looking for her lost sheep. Turns out, Allie was close by. The two girls lived in the same neighborhood and went to the same school. Allie didn't know much about Jesus, but she was open. Fast forward several weeks (and several trips to the local coffee shop) and the lost sheep was found! One conversation led to another, and, by the power of the Holy Spirit, Allie came to believe that she is a beloved, forgiven daughter of the heavenly King. Woohoo!

Kaitlyn then asked, "Have you been baptized?" "What's baptism?" Allie asked back. And the conversation continued.

Eventually, however, Allie's baptism was scheduled, and I am grateful it was on the Sunday I was there. As I witnessed her being baptized, I could almost hear Jesus calling out, "Rejoice with me; I have found my lost sheep!" And the congregation did, clapping and rejoicing as she stood there newly baptized with a huge smile on her face!

Once I was at a church in Nebraska when a dad came up to me and said, "I wasn't sure about this 'joining Jesus' thing. But I decided what could it hurt to start looking for my 'one.' Then, out of the blue, one of the guys at work was diagnosed with cancer. Instead of avoiding him, like I would've done before, I started checking in with him. He's divorced, so as he got sicker, I offered to stop by his home and sit with him, run errands for him, stuff like that. I met his two kids. They're about the same age as mine – early teens. After a few visits, our conversation turned to faith. In fact, he brought it up. He had been raised a Christian but had drifted away years ago. The cancer had him thinking a lot about God again. And he had questions. So, we talked. I guess he had somehow missed the message of God's grace because, when I told him what the Bible says, his faith came back strong.

"Then, a couple months ago, he asked me if I thought his kids could go with mine to youth group. I said, 'Sure.' And guess what? Next Sunday they're being baptized. Isn't that cool? Would you like to meet them? They're right over there."

As I met them, I could almost hear Jesus calling out, "Rejoice with me; I have found my lost sheep!" Even though I wouldn't be there to witness their baptism the next week, I could certainly imagine the clapping and rejoicing that would erupt both in the church and in heaven!

Like we said, it really is a pretty fun way to live.

However, sometimes the search doesn't go quite as quickly. I was in Oregon speaking at a conference and an elderly woman approached me. She asked if I was related to any Finkes in San Francisco. I said, "Not that I know of. Why do you ask?" She replied, "When I was a girl, my family lived next door to a couple named Finke. I wasn't a Christian at the time. However, our families enjoyed spending time together, and eventually the Finkes invited me to go to church with them. After that, I went with them nearly every Sunday until I finished eighth grade, when my dad took a new job and we moved away. I never saw the Finkes again. At the time of our move, I still hadn't become a Christian. In fact, it took several more years, but because of the seeds the Finkes planted, the Lord finally caught me," she said with a smile. "I only wish they could have known..."

Somehow, I think they probably do. After all, Jesus said, "I tell you that in the same way there will be more rejoicing in heaven over one sinner who repents than over ninety-nine righteous persons who do not need to repent."

Now, here's the question for your family: Who's *your* "one?" Who in your neighborhood, daycare, school, or workplace is struggling without the grace and truth of Jesus? Surely there are many but start with one. Is it one child? One family? Does each of your family members have their own "one?" Whatever the answer, you won't find your "one" unless you actually start looking.

So, how do you actually start?

Pray.

Pray that God would help you find your "one." He knows who they are and where to look.

As a family, brainstorm low-risk, fun ways to meet the children, families, and neighbors around you so you can start looking for the ones who need a little grace and truth.

What are their names? What are their stories? What does God seem to be up to in their lives?

One way to meet people and start looking for your "one" is to do what Jesus is doing in Luke 15, "This man welcomes sinners and eats with them." In other words, share some food, share some laughs, share some stories. Jesus certainly endorses this strategy. In fact, he was known for it! (See Luke 5:29, 7:36, 15:2, Matthew 11:19, 22:8-10, John 12:2.)

Jesus was known for eating dinners with sinners. And why did Jesus use that approach to look for the lost? Because it worked so well! While having an unhurried meal together, Jesus could show he valued them, ask them questions, learn their stories, and then share his own.

Of course, looking for your "one" doesn't have to include food.

The point is to meet the children, families, or neighbors God has placed around you and find out who they are. What is a low-risk, fun way your family can get started?

Identify your "one."

Ultimately, how do you know who your "one" is? Look for the child, family, or neighbor who is ready to receive your family's friendship.

WHO'S YOUR ONE? = WHO'S READY?

Not everyone will be ready to connect in friendship. And that's okay. In Luke 10:6 Jesus says not to worry about who isn't ready. Instead, look for the one who is.

And then make it a family priority to offer love and friendship to your "one."

You're not writing off the other 99 around you. Love them too. But *prioritize* your one.

- As a family, identify your values and write them down so that whenever you interact with your "one" you provide a fun, safe environment with healthy boundaries.
- If you are uncomfortable with what your children may be exposed to when they visit other homes, make it simple for your children to invite their "one" to your home.
- During visits, don't hover, but be attentive.
- Be interested in who they are.
- Let them experience a little of what your family already has in abundance: Jesus' love, joy, peace, patience, kindness, goodness, faithfulness, gentleness, and self-control.

- Let them see how your family interacts. How you resolve differences, offer forgiveness, and treat each other with grace.
- If they are with you during "Circle Up" time, invite them to participate.
- Afterwards, debrief with your children. Don't grill them but invite their reflections. What happened? What was Jesus up to? Highlight the little things. And pray together for the seeds that were just sown.

So, who's your "one" and when will you start looking? Because there's a celebration to be had.

HERE'S THE POINT

To take "joining Jesus" to the next level, your family will want to do one more thing Jesus does: prioritize lost sheep. Who is your family's one lost sheep? What's their name? What's their story? What's Jesus already up to in their life?

SUSAN'S SNIPPETS

We enjoyed opening our home to the friends of our kids and practicing hospitality. We wanted everyone to feel welcome. For years we had a saying displayed in our entryway, "Enter as Guests, Leave as Friends." At the same time, keeping our discipling rhythms when other kids were in the house kept us accountable and authentic.

For instance, that meant our fifth-grade daughter might be embarrassed that we still had bedtime prayers when her friend was staying overnight. (The friend's mother shared that the prayer made quite an impression and sparked meaningful conversations at home.)

A high school boy who was interested in our daughter spent many meals with us because our daughter was not allowed to go to his unsupervised home. Yes, he knew this was the only way he could be with her, but that's okay. He also got to be a part of many family conversations where he heard about Jesus being a normal part of our lives.

Another friend came from a cultural background which preferred certain kinds of foods. "Are you eating with us tonight?" I'd ask. "Well, what are you having?" she'd reply. Then depending on my answer, she'd sometimes ask, "Can I just sit with you and not eat?" She enjoyed different foods than we were able to provide, but she enjoyed being a part of the family conversations we had around our table.

Board game nights and cookie baking nights regularly took place in our home with a diverse group of high school kids. It left the kitchen messy, but the laughter and conversation were worth it. Over the years, we often saw rolled eyes from our daughters, but looking back I think they enjoyed having their friends see who we were as a family. Seeds sown. Celebrations to be had.

CHAPTER 17

BUILDING YOUR FAMILY'S VILLAGE: PEERS, MENTORS, AND PROFESSIONALS

"Omwana ni wa bhone."
Roughly translated, "It takes a village to raise a child."

— a Wajita/Tanzanian proverb

In various East African cultures, there is a parenting proverb that is translated something like this, "It takes a village to raise a child."

Insightful. Spot-on.

Yes, parents are primarily responsible for raising their own children. Yes, they lay the all-important foundation. However, experience shows – and numerous studies validate – that as children grow, they benefit tremendously when they also have a "village" of people surrounding them who can verify, reinforce, and expand upon the foundation the parents are laying.

That's why, as you round out your plan for discipling your children, it is wise to be *intentional* about who will make up your family's village. Who are the people you want to regularly influence your children? Who can verify, reinforce, and expand upon the foundation you are laying?

Ideally, a village will include relationships with extended family, peers, non-parent mentors, ministry professionals and volunteers. The idea isn't to surround your children with people who look, think, and act like you. Rather, the idea is to have your children regularly interact with people who *believe* like you, but bring a variety of personalities, perspectives, ethnicities, and generations into your family's village of relationships.

Here's how it works. When your children are small, they watch you, believe you, and want to become like you. You are their unrivaled hero. However, as they grow, they start looking around to see if others agree with your family's beliefs and lifestyle. It's not bad. It's just their next step of growing up. They're looking for verification. They're looking for reinforcement. They're looking for more information.

So, make sure they find it. How?

By building them a "village" of relationships where they regularly interact with peers and adults who see themselves as trainees of Jesus too: not just church-goers but Jesus-followers; not just people who worship Jesus on Sundays, but who get up off their pews and join Jesus on his mission in daily life; not just people who study the faith but who have stories about what happens when they live the faith for the good of others (see 1 Thessalonians 2:8).

Include people who regularly verify and reinforce the importance of affirming one another's true identity, value, and purpose in Christ; people who are living fruitful and fulfilling lives because they have learned to trust the Father courageously, humble themselves authentically, and offer his love generously; people who aren't afraid of your children asking hard questions and addressing nagging doubts because they know it's part of growing up and growing stronger (see Hebrews 13:7).

Let's be clear: the goal of your village is not to insulate your children from worldly influences; but, as they get older, to provide the support and input they need from a variety of Jesus-followers who can help them process those influences within the framework of faith.

So, who will be in your family's village? Let's get started.

Peers

In passages like Psalm 1:1-6, Proverbs 22:24-25, and Philippians 3:15-17, the Bible highlights what we all experienced as children: making friends with peers who are good influences leads to good while making friends with peers who are "mockers," "wicked," and "those who are hot-tempered" only "corrupts good character" (1 Corinthians 15:33). I still remember the peers who were good for me as I was growing up and those who were not so good for me.

Bottom line? It was just so much easier to choose the path that followed Jesus when I had friends heading that way too.

So, who are those peers for your children? Identify them and be intentional about bringing them into your children's village so friendships can form and deepen. Maximize the unhurried time they spend together so they influence each other for good. Invite them along on your family mission adventures so they have shared Jesus-stories with your children. For instance, invite them to come along as you serve in an under-served community, or as you cross the street to bless a person who needs a hand, or as you host a block party to look for lost sheep, or as you reach out to welcome a new neighbor. Invite them to join in the fun of looking around, taking note, and recognizing where there are adventures to be had with Jesus.

Having said that, maximizing time with peers who follow Jesus doesn't mean eliminating time with peers who do not. Include them too. In fact, Jesus would say make them a priority, right? (See the previous chapter.) By providing opportunities for them to spend unhurried time with your children and their Jesus-following friends, you are helping them to experience fun, laughter, and conversation in the midst of the fruit of the Spirit. And that is *very* influential.

Mentors, Other Parents, and Extended Family

While peers certainly have an important impact on a child's development, studies show (perhaps surprisingly) that an even greater impact is made when a child has a number of supportive, engaged relationships with non-parent adults. (Search online for studies by Gallop, Barna, or the Search Institute.)

These kinds of relationships become especially important as children enter their preteen years and beyond. For instance, according to research published in 2020, adolescents who have supportive, engaged relationships with non-parent adults, enjoy better mental, spiritual, and even physical health during their young adult years than adolescents who do not have such relationships.

Who are "non-parent adults?" They include the following:

> Extended family – grandparents, uncles or aunts, older cousins
> Teachers, coaches, directors, neighbors, small group leaders, youth workers, or pastors
> Parents of your children's friends
> Family friends

The studies even suggest the number of relationships to aim for: at least five. And more is better. In other words, the more adults they have pouring into their lives – both affirming them and challenging them – the better they do.

Makes sense.

Again, parents lay the foundation which remains for a lifetime. But as children grow, they need other adults they respect to verify, reinforce, and build upon the foundation their parents are laying. In my preteen years, my mom and dad could tell me things over and over again and, although I would comply, I would do so essentially rolling my eyes. But if Mr. Garman said *the exact same thing* (or Mrs. Keys or Mr. Fritsche or one of my aunts or uncles), I was suddenly convinced. It wasn't that I disbelieved my parents, I just needed a little verification. I bet you have similar stories.

So, who will be in your family's village of relationships? Think of a combination of diverse adults who already love your children and follow Jesus as a daily adventure. What are their names and when will you talk with them about joining your family's village?

Church Professionals and Ministry Volunteers

A third group to consider for your family's "village" is the pastor, ministry professional(s), and volunteers from your church. After all, they are already offering biblical teaching and programming to your family on a weekly basis.

However, while including them may seem like an obvious choice for church-going parents, I offer a caution. Although it is indeed wise for you to team up with your church to disciple your children, you will need to resist the common temptation to *turn over* your children's discipleship to them.

TEAM UP FOR DISCIPLESHIP? YES.
TURN OVER DISCIPLESHIP? NO.

Here's what I mean.

According to nationwide research conducted by the Barna Group, 85%

of Christian parents believe they have the primary responsibility for raising (discipling) their children to be followers of Jesus. On its face, this sounds like a good thing, right? Parents are acknowledging their responsibility.

Unfortunately, the research also found that a majority of the 85% assume they are fulfilling that responsibility by taking their children to church for an hour or two per week. Again, on its face, taking children to church sounds good. Except the research also found that a majority of parents who assume they are fulfilling their responsibility by taking their children to church then spend *little or no time during the rest of the week talking with their children about spiritual matters.*

This means a majority of parents assume the professionals and volunteers at church will be able to raise their children to be followers of Jesus *for them.* But it simply doesn't work that way. What parents do day by day, week after week makes a far deeper impression on their children – for better or worse – than what the church can accomplish in an hour or two once a week. (Thus, my caution earlier.)

There are two main reasons this is so:

1. How your children are designed by God
2. The sheer number of hours your children spend with you vs. the professionals and volunteers at church

Your children are designed by God to watch, imitate, and become a version of you. Which means it's an unsound strategy for you to send your children to church hoping they will somehow become a version of their pastor or youth director instead. It's not how God designed discipleship to work.

Are there exceptions? Sure. I often hear heartening stories from people who, by God's grace, have overcome an anemic spiritual upbringing to become passionate followers of Jesus. And often there is a youth director or a children's ministry volunteer in the story. But for every story that ends like that there are many, many more that end with the person just walking away.

So, why put your children in that position in the first place? Instead, write the better story.

Take a deep breath and trust God. You are the one he chose to raise and disciple your children. Enjoy showing them how to live a fruitful and fulfilling life of love. Enjoy the ups and downs of writing the better story with them. Like many parents, you may be tempted to think ministry professionals and volunteers can do a better job than you, that they're smarter, godlier, and more talented than you. But there's just one problem with that line of thinking.

They're not you.

And your children need *you*. That's how God designed them.

The people at church can and will help you, but they can't replace you.

Which brings us to the second reason the people at church can't raise your children to be followers of Jesus for you: time.

Studies show even the most active church families are only able to invest about 40 hours per year in church programming (even though churches may offer more than 150 hours). On the other hand, children spend 3000 hours per year with their families. (3000 is the number of hours families have after subtracting eight hours of sleep per day and eight hours of school per day.)

40 VS. 3000

Wow. That's not even close. Families have the opportunity to spend *75 times* more hours together than they do with ministry professionals and volunteers. That's an overwhelming difference.

What's your family doing with all that time?

Several years ago, I was preaching a series of messages on Deuteronomy

6:6-7, "These commandments that I give you today are to be upon your hearts. Impress them on your children. Talk about them when you sit at home and when you walk along the road, when you lie down and when you get up."

In one of the messages, I wanted to illustrate for parents the difference between the number of hours our church volunteers had with their children versus the number of hours they had. To do that, I borrowed 3040 tennis balls from the tennis club as well as several shopping carts from the grocery store. I filled the carts with the 3000 tennis balls (representing the hours families had) and put the remaining 40 tennis balls in a clear plastic bag (representing the hours the church had).

At the right moment in the message, I signaled my team to wheel out the shopping carts one after the other. I can't remember how many carts there were but there were *a lot*. I then stood among the carts, holding up the remaining 40 tennis balls. The obvious difference was striking and made my point.

But I'm a preacher, so I kept preaching.

I said, "As a congregation, we are blessed with talented ministry staff and volunteers who do an amazing job with our children. Amen? (There was heartfelt applause.) But let's be honest. The score is 40 to 3000. As talented and committed as they are, we can't expect them to overcome in an hour on Sunday what our children are seeing in us, hearing from us, and experiencing with us hour after hour the rest of the week."

The point, of course, wasn't to make anyone feel bad. The point was to help everyone wake up. It's not smart to expect your church's professionals and volunteers to disciple your children for you. It just doesn't work. But here's what *does* work:

- Faithful participation in weekly services and programming so the ministry professionals and volunteers have an opportunity to verify, reinforce, and expand upon the foundation you are laying with your children.

- During "Circle Up" time, talk with your children about the teaching, preaching, and programming they have experienced. For example, ask, "What did you learn from God's Word today? How can we put it into practice this week?"
- Enjoy an occasional meal with the ministry staff or volunteers who work directly with your family so you can get to know them personally and hear their Jesus-stories.

A few months ago, while I was still drafting this chapter, Susan and I returned to Midland, Michigan to conduct the funeral of a friend. We had led a church there for 18 years. I had been the senior pastor, and Susan led the family ministry staff. Our late friend was part of a large extended family, most of whom had been connected with our church. And everyone was there – four generations.

Our family had moved away 14 years earlier when most of the children of this extended family had been in middle school or younger. We had occasionally visited Midland over the years but hadn't seen the children until now. Susan and I were both surprised and delighted as we watched the "children" walking in with children of their own!

Despite the occasion, it was a wonderful reunion. Susan and I caught up with friends who are now grandparents and with their "children" who are now raising children of their own. The absolute best part was learning that the "children" are still followers of Jesus and that they are raising their children to be followers of Jesus too.

The impact which one generation can have on the next was obvious in the room. The foundation of love and faith laid by the parents and grandparents was clear throughout these four generations.

As the "children" reminisced with us, they also told us how important it had been for them to grow up in a church with ministry staff, mentors, and other parents who could pour into them each week. All these years later, they could still remember certain songs, teachings, conversations and experiences. There was no replacing the deep bedrock of love and faith their families had laid day by day. But their stories were evidence of how the teaching and programming of our church had indeed served as an important supplement for verifying, reinforcing, and expanding upon the bedrock that was laid.

The score wasn't 40 vs. 3000, but 3000 + 40.

And it worked.

Just before we had to leave, I took a moment to stand back from the crowd and take it all in. I thought about all the conversations I had had during the day and about this chapter I was still writing. It occurred to me that this room full of joyful Jesus-followers was indeed tangible proof that it really does take a village to raise a child.

One Last Parenting Tool for Your Toolbox: "Circle Up" for the Village

Around the country, Susan and I know many young families who utilize a parenting tool they call their "Missional Community." They regularly gather with other families in their village to share a meal and then share their stories of how life on mission with Jesus is going (both the ups and the downs). They sort through what God is teaching them in his Word and showing them in everyday life. They encourage each other, offer insights to each other, spur each other on to another week of joining Jesus on his mission, and they pray for each other (see Hebrews 10:24-25 and 13:7).

If this sounds familiar, it's because a "Missional Community" follows the same general format as the family "Circle Up" time we advocated in chapter 15:

> Invite Jesus-stories by asking questions.
>
> Read the gospels together.
>
> Identify what Jesus is giving us to believe and do heading into the new week.
>
> Help each other with prayer.

It also serves the same general purpose: helping people reframe all that happens with Jesus' grace, truth, and mission in the middle of it. The only real difference between "Circle Up" and "Missional Community" is that the group is expanded beyond the immediate family to include at least a subset of their village.

For these families, a "Missional Community" doesn't replace their "Circle Up" time at home. Their "Missional Community" is more like their next circle out.

Susan and I followed a similar practice when our children were young. We had daily "Circle Up" time as a family, and then gathered weekly with our "Missional Community." Because life was busy, our "Missional Community" was the best way to assure our children could spend consistent time with at least a subset of our village. Besides, they considered this time together the highlight of their week, and they were always disappointed if we had to miss it.

Last but certainly not least, as your children grow into adolescence, you can help them continue reinforcing and expanding their foundation of faith by encouraging them to form a "Missional Community" of their own.

For instance, when one of our children was in middle school, she recruited peers from her public school to start one. She wasn't ready to leave behind our daily "Circle Ups," but she *was* ready for the next circle out. We asked a college-aged woman from our village to help facilitate, and she eagerly agreed. Together the group laughed, shared Jesus-stories, and even shared some tears. They read God's Word, sorted through questions they had, and helped each other in prayer. Together, they encouraged each other, gained insight from each other, and spurred each other on to follow Jesus and join him on his mission.

In short, they found what I had found when I was their age: it is so much easier to choose the path that follows Jesus when you have friends heading that way too.

HERE'S THE POINT

While it is parents who lay the foundation of love and faith for their children, as the children grow, they benefit tremendously when they have a "village" of people surrounding them who can verify, reinforce, and expand upon the foundation the parents are laying. So, as you round out your plan for discipling your children, it is wise to be *intentional* about who will make up your family's village. Who are the people you want to regularly influence your children? Who can verify, reinforce, and expand upon the foundation you are laying?

SUSAN'S SNIPPETS

Over the years, we have been blessed to have very special people in our kids' "village." Some have continued to be strong, positive influences even though our kids are adults. Some have journeyed with us even though miles separated us. Some were in a new neighborhood that became a new, strong village for our family.

"Kasserian Ingera," is a traditional greeting between the Maasai people of East Africa. It means, "How are the children?" Even people who do not have their own children answer, "All the children are well," because they know the village has to work together to care for and nurture their children. The village is well if their children are well.

We thank the Lord for the village he provided us even as we pray that we may be part of a spiritually influential village for other families as well. And may your family have both the blessing of a village surrounding you and the privilege of being a part of someone else's village.

BENEDICTION

"May the favor of the Lord our God rest upon us;
and establish the work of our hands for us
– yes, establish the work of our hands."
Psalm 90:17

Jesus shows parents how to raise our children to be his followers:

Jesus' discipling goal for our children:
...to live a life of love as they join him on his mission

Jesus' three discipling priorities for our children:
...to be convinced that he redeemed and restored their true
identity, value, and purpose
...to have increasing capacity for trusting the Father more and
humbling themselves faster so that they can offer his love more
generously
...to have growing ability for using the Five Mission Practices
in their daily life

Jesus' discipling rhythm for our children:
...to weave his priorities into their daily life by teaching them,
showing them, sending them, and circling up with them to
share the stories

Yes, a lot is at stake. Yes, you need to keep your eye on the ball and do your best. But you've got this, my friend. You really do. You've got this because *Jesus has got you*. He's already set you up to succeed because he's already given you the most important ingredient for raising your children: his love.

And his love makes all the difference.

His love neither takes the adventure out of parenting nor guarantees that your children won't take a walk through the valley of the shadow of death (Psalm 23:4). But his love does mean he will remain relentlessly faithful to your family until he has worked all things together for your good and his purpose (Romans 8:28).

Remember, Jesus isn't asking you for your flawless perfection, only your humble participation. You bring the water. He turns it into wine.

So, let's get started.

Receive the blessing of the Lord: In the name of the Father, whose favor rests upon you; in the name of the Son, who has redeemed you, restored you, and shown you what to do; in the name of the Holy Spirit, who establishes the work of your hands – yes, who establishes the work of your hands especially in the lives of your children. Amen.

SUSAN'S SNIPPETS

Amen! Now, keep it simple, be intentional, and go have some fun joining Jesus as a family!

APPENDIX

DISCUSSION GUIDE FOR PARENTS

The following guide divides the book into 10 sessions. It is designed to help both groups and individuals process their insights and, just as importantly, turn those insights into action for the benefit of their families. Under the title of each session, you will find the chapter(s) that will be covered. If participants haven't had time to read, they can quickly review the "Here's the Point" paragraph(s) at the end of each chapter. A Bible passage is also provided to serve as the foundation for your discussion.

We recommend that you leave enough time at the conclusion of your gatherings to do the suggested "Wrap Up" exercises. You may also want to choose a key insight or question from your discussion for continued reflection and journaling on your own. Journaling is simply writing down your thoughts and feelings as a way to sort through them. The practice may help you gain clarity for what Jesus is giving you to believe and do as you raise your children. Don't forget to download more resources to use with your family. They are free and available at www.dwelling114.org.

Enjoy!

Session 1

What Does It Mean to Disciple My Child?   By EXSAMPLÉ

Chapters 1-2

Matthew 4:19

Philippians 3:17

1. Introduce your family to the group by sharing their names, ages, and one compliment about each.

2. What are you hoping to gain from this book?

3. In chapter one, Greg describes the reaction parents had when he told them the goal of the book is "to help parents intentionally disciple their kids to become lifelong followers of Jesus."

    What is your reaction to that goal? Are you terrified, excited, incredulous, or something else? Why?

4. As you read Greg's conversation with the group, what "light bulbs" clicked on?

    Was there a key phrase or quote that got your attention? Share it with the group.

    If your children are older, as you read the conversation, what would you underscore for parents who have younger children?
    HOW IMPORTANT 13 - 16 AGE TO TITHER
    BE WARE

5. Before reading chapter two, how would you have defined the words "disciple" and "discipleship"?

How would you define them now?

6. God wired the child/parent relationship so that raising your
    child = discipling your child. In other words, your lifestyle is
    your child's discipleship curriculum, for better or worse.

    If you were raised in a Christian home, what kind of Jesus-
    followers were your parents? Apathetic? Duty-driven? Harsh
    and overbearing? Fruitful and fulfilled? Something else?

    How has their example affected the way you are raising your
    children to be Jesus-followers?

    If you weren't raised in a Christian home, what did your parents
    think about Christians? *SUBjECT NEVER CAME*

    How has their example affected the way you are raising your
    children to be Jesus-followers? *WHEN OUR CHILDREN WERE*
    15-16 - WE WERE OVER INVOLVED IN CHURCH
    OUR SON ~OID FOLLOWER ~US

7.   What are some ways you can be more intentional about being
     the kind of Jesus-follower you want your children to see and
     imitate?

Wrap Up

What insights came to you during this session? How can you
immediately put the insights into action to benefit your family?
(Remember, whatever Jesus gives you to do, he enables you to do by grace.)

Is there an insight or question on which you want to continue
reflecting and journaling?

Go around the group and ask, "How can we help each other in prayer?" Then have each person or couple pray for the next.

Session 2
Parenting with the End in Mind
Chapters 3-4

John 13:35
Ephesians 5:1-2

1. Can you remember the first time Jesus and your faith became real to you? Share your story with the group.

2. As you read chapters three and four, what stood out for you?

3. If you feel your child is becoming bored, unfulfilled, and unconvinced of the Christian life, what can you do to help them?

4. Because your child is following you through the weeds of this world, it's important for you to be clear about where are you leading. So, where are you leading and is that where you want your child to end up?

5. What meaning does the following quote have for you? "You can't go back and change the beginning, but you can start where you are and change the ending."

6. The Finkes tell the story of their whitewater rafting experience. What was the difference between their daughter's experience and their own?

7. In what specific ways can you "take your child on the ride with Jesus"?

8. Chapter four begins by having parents ask themselves, "Because my child is learning how to live life from me, how then shall I live?" How does God answer the question? (Hint, Ephesians 5:2.)

9. How would you define "love"? What does it look like to "live a life of love"?

    Which of the many Bible passages quoted in chapter four resonated with you? Why?

10. Jesus died on the cross and rose again to take away your sin and to restore your ability "to will and to act according to his purpose," (Philippians 2:13). So, if you struggle to consistently live a life of love, it's not because you lack Jesus' power or capability. What are you lacking?

    Jesus will show us how to remedy that in the next chapter.

Wrap Up

What insights came to you during this session? How can you immediately put the insights into action to benefit your family? (Remember, whatever Jesus gives you to do, he enables you to do by grace.)

Is there an insight or question on which you want to continue reflecting and journaling?

Go around the group and ask, "How can we help each other in prayer?" Then have each person or couple pray for the next.

Session 3
How to Join Jesus in Discipling Your Family
Chapter 5

Proverbs 24:3
1. Describe your family in six words or less.

2. Review the two questions you answered in Session 2 and share any insights, which have emerged since you last met:

    "Where do I want my children to end up?"
    Imitating Jesus and living an abundant, generous life of love as they join him on his mission.

    "To lead my children there, how then shall I live?"
    I will set the example by imitating Jesus myself and living an abundant, generous life of love as I join him on his mission.

3. In chapter five, the Finkes introduce the question that will take up most of the rest of the book:

    "What is Jesus' discipling process and is there a simple way my family can weave it into our daily lives so we get better at living a life of love and joining Jesus on his mission?"

As a group, list Jesus' three discipling priorities and his discipling rhythm.

4. What about this list makes sense to you? What questions do you still have?

5. The chapter concludes with a message of encouragement for parents. How would you summarize this message?

Wrap Up

What insights came to you during this session? How can you immediately put the insights into action to benefit your family? (Remember, whatever Jesus gives you to do, he enables you to do by grace.)

Is there an insight or question on which you want to continue reflecting and journaling?

Go around the group and ask, "How can we help each other in prayer?" Then have each person or couple pray for the next.

Session 4
True Identity: Jesus' #1 Discipling Priority
Chapters 6-9

1 John 3:1

1. Share a story of what happened as you put one of your insights from last time into action to benefit your family.

2. Jesus died on the cross and rose again to take away your family's sin and to restore your true identity, value, and purpose.

Because of Jesus, what is your true identity? "We are..."

Because of Jesus, what do you have of value to offer others? "We have..."

Because of Jesus, what is your true purpose every day? "We get to..."

3. The Finkes refer to "the things of the Kingdom" as superpowers from God. Why are things like love, joy, and kindness superpowers?

4. Why is it important to raise your children to be convinced of their true identity, value, and purpose? How will that benefit them?

5. As parents, you not only want your children to know these truths in their heads, but to be convinced of them in their hearts. According to Jesus, how can you make that connection between your children's heads and hearts?

6. What does it mean to "practice remembering"?

As a group, write a draft of a family cheer-creed.

Later, at home, write one with your family and have fun making it your own.

7. Do you agree that experiencing love = feeling valued? Why or why not?

8. For better or worse, children experience the Father's love most tangibly through their parents, and that experience deeply affects their ability to understand and trust his love as they grow into adulthood.

   How has the way you experienced love through your parents affected how you understand and trust the Father's love today?

9. Is it easy or not so easy for you to express unconditional love to your children?

   What can you do to demonstrate unconditional love to your children in a more intentional and consistent way?

Wrap Up

What insights came to you during this session? How can you immediately put the insights into action to benefit your family? (Remember, whatever Jesus gives you to do, he enables you to do by grace.)

Is there an insight or question on which you want to continue reflecting and journaling?

Go around the group and ask, "How can we help each other in prayer?" Then have each person or couple pray for the next.

Session 5

Increased Capacity: Trusting the Father More

Chapters 10-11

Matthew 10:8b

1. Remind each other of what your true identity, value, and purpose are because of Jesus.

   For fun, share the cheer-creed your family wrote.

2. Share a story of what happened as you put one of your insights from last time into action to benefit your family.

3. Jesus' "next level of training" focuses on three discipling priorities for his followers. What are they? *TRUSTING THE FATHER HUMBLING THEM SELF EASIER OFFERING LOVE MORE COURAGEOUSLY + GENEROUSLY*
   Why is it necessary to increase these capacities? How will they benefit your children? *THE MORE THEY WILL THRIVE AND SERVE JESUS*

4. What did you like in chapter eleven's discussion about raising courageous boys and girls?

   What was challenging?

5. Is there a difference between faith and trust? If so, what do you think it is? *TRUST IS LEARDED FAITH IS BELIEVING IS GIFT*

6. The Finkes share a number of stories about their children, Peter and Jesus, and building more trust in the Father. Which one resonated with you and why?

7. "Scary" is in the eye of the beholder and looks different at different ages. Share a story about when one of your children faced something hard and scary with courage.

    How can you use this story to continue building their capacity for trust and courage?

Wrap Up

What insights came to you during this session? How can you immediately put the insights into action to benefit your family? (Remember, whatever Jesus gives you to do, he enables you to do by grace.)

Go around the group and ask, "How can we help each other in prayer?" Then have each person or couple pray for the next.

Session 6

Increased Capacity: Humbling Themselves Faster

Chapters 12-13 14

1 Peter 5:5-7

1. Use your family cheer-creed to remind each other of what your true identity, value, and purpose are because of Jesus.

2. Review what Jesus' discipling priorities include.

3. Tell a story of what happened as you put one of your insights from last time into action to benefit your family.

4. What got your attention as you read this chapter about humility and confidence?   How Hard it is Live up to That Standard

5. Why is humility important to practice as you join Jesus on his mission?

6. Why does biblical humility result in confident children?

7. How do people learn to be humble?

8. Share a story about when one of your children showed humility.

   How can you use this story to help them continue building their capacity for humility?

9. Together, review "How to Apply Jesus' Framework with Our Children". Which of the four points is an area of growth for you?

Wrap Up

What insights came to you during this session? How can you immediately put the insights into action to benefit your family? (Remember, whatever Jesus gives you to do, he enables you to do by grace.)

Go around the group and ask, "How can we help each other in prayer?" Then have each person or couple pray for the next.

Session 7

Growing Ability: Discipling Your Children to Use Their Superpower
Chapter 14

Luke 6:40

1. Share a story of what happened as you put one of your insights from last time into action to benefit your family.

2. Review what Jesus' discipling priorities include.

3. As you read this chapter, what "light bulbs" came on for you?

4. Why is God's love your family's superpower?

5. Have you seen God's love change a person? Share that story with the group.

6. Jesus grows his followers' ability to use their superpower by working on five mission skills.

    What are the five skills? (Susan has a two-minute video online to help you remember. Go to www.dwelling114.org, click the "Training Tools" dropdown menu, click "Joining Jesus as a Family," and scroll down to the video button.)

7. Look at the five mission skills and tell a story about how your family has put one of them into practice. What did you do? How did it go? What did you learn?

Wrap Up

Over the next few days, what is a low-risk baby step your family can take to show love to someone?

Go around the group and ask, "How can we help each other in prayer?" Then have each person or couple pray for the next.

Session 8

Jesus' Discipling Rhythm: Teach, Show, Send, and Circle Up

Chapter 15

Deuteronomy 6:4-7

1. Share a story of what happened as you put one of your insights from last time into action to benefit your family.

2. As you read about Jesus' discipling rhythm in chapter fifteen, what were your take-aways?

3. Which piece of the rhythm do the Finkes say is the key to the whole thing?

    Why will the conversations of your "Circle Up" time be so important?

4. In the gospels, Jesus' days were busy and his schedule was full. However, he made discipling his followers his priority.

    If you want discipleship to become your family's priority, what decisions about how you manage time need to be made?

5. How will you weave Jesus' discipling rhythm into your family's daily life? Describe what a typical day could look like from morning to bedtime.

6. What was the discipleship rhythm of your family as you grew up?

    What lessons can you apply as you seek to disciple your family?

Wrap Up

Have each person or couple in the group commit to having "Circle Up" times with their children over the next several days. Be ready to share your experiences the next time you gather.

Go around the group and ask, "How can we help each other in prayer?" Then have each person or couple pray for the next.

Session 9

Joining Jesus on His Mission: Who's Your One?

Chapter 16

Luke 15:1-7

1. Share a story about what happened during your family's "Circle Up" times.

    What went well? What did you learn? What will you do differently going forward?

2. To take "Joining Jesus" to the next level, your family will want to do something Jesus does. What is it?

3. Your family's job isn't to save lost sheep (the Bible says you can't even save yourself), but you can look for lost sheep. How did Jesus look for lost sheep? (Hint: what was he accused of doing in Luke 15:2?)

    How can your family look for lost sheep?

4. Can you name a person or family who is your family's one lost sheep? In other words, who's your "one?"

5. By meeting the people around you, you will be in position to start looking for the ones who need a little of God's grace and truth.

    As a group, brainstorm some low-risk, fun ways to meet the children, families, and neighbors God has already placed around you. (Several ideas are listed in our book, "Joining Jesus on His Mission," pages 149-151.)

6. What seems challenging to you about offering love and friendship to your family's "one"?

    What are some ideas to keep your children safe as they spend time with their "one"?

Wrap Up

Have each person or couple in the group commit to developing a plan with their children for seeking the lost sheep around them. Be ready to share your progress next time.

Go around the group and ask, "How can we help each other in prayer?" Then have each person or couple pray for the next.

Session 10
Building Your Family's Village: Peers, Mentors, and Professionals
Chapter 17

Philippians 4:9

1. Share a story about what happened during your family's recent "Circle Up" times.

    What went well? What did you learn? What will you do differently going forward?

2. What's your family's plan for joining Jesus on his mission and meeting the children, families, neighbors around you? What progress have you made?

3. As you read about building your family's village, what seemed particularly important?

4. Do you already have a village? If so, who are they?

    Who are people you would like to invite, and how would you go about inviting them?

5. What's the difference between "teaming up" versus "turning over" your children's discipleship to church professionals and volunteers?

6. The Finkes introduced the idea of a Missional Community. What is a Missional Community?

As your group has been meeting, you have essentially been functioning as a Missional Community. What have been some benefits in meeting regularly?

Would you like to continue meeting as a Missional Community?

If your children are older, how can you help them start their own Missional Community?

Wrap Up

What insights came to you during this session? How can you immediately put the insights into action to benefit your family? (Remember, whatever Jesus gives you to do, he enables you to do by grace.)

Go around the group and ask, "How can we help each other in prayer?" Then have each person or couple pray for the next.

Neighborhood Prayer Map

dwelling 1:14

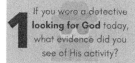
If you were a detective **looking for God** today, what evidence did you see of His activity?

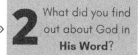
What did you find out about God in **His Word**?

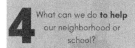
What can we do **to help** our neighborhood or school?

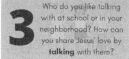
Who do you like talking with at school or in your neighborhood? How can you share Jesus' love by **talking** with them?

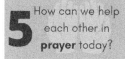
How can we help each other in **prayer** today?

THE Questions!